RELATIONAL WEALTH

Why Relationships Are The
World's Real Capital

Betty Murambadoro

Acknowledgements

All glory to God for His word that is anchored on relationships and all elements that enhance it. For years, I have yearned to develop a deeper relationship with Him and meaningful relationships with those that He positions in my life.

As you turn the pages of this book, you will gather insights of the amazing yet very touching life of my late mother, Ottilia Moyo. From her, I gathered deep life lessons on how to make a marked difference in relationship management.

Heartfelt gratitude to Dr Vongai Nyahunzvi, who championed the weaving of the chapters of this book together and unpacking my relationship management journey in a manner I never imagined possible. Thank you for your selflessness and heart to serve.

Sincere gratitude to the Financial Gazette for publication of the thirteen articles, at the time of writing this book. These articles formed the very foundation upon which this book is anchored. To my two marketplace sisters,

Tariro Memo and Tendai Rafemoyo, I am in awe at how I got to thirteen articles, with you cheering me on.

My siblings, my bloodline, the Moyo clan, what a journey we shared, marred with momentary celebration but with roots of pain and yearning for a better tomorrow. Through it all, we are still standing and more refined in navigating relationships in a unique way.

Special thanks to Patrick for sharing lifelong experiences with me on what credits or debits the "relational capital account". To our children, Mufaro, Manatsa and Mukundi, thank you for who you are becoming as you embrace the value behind being relational. Relationships will always triumph over transactions. Journey on and develop high-impact relationships across all societal structures.

Special acknowledgement to Pastors Tom and Bonnie Deuschle for the years invested in teaching me character and genuine connection.

Foreword

I met Betty Murambadoro through her writing. A good friend and young sister forwarded me one of her articles from the *Financial Gazette*, a piece about relationships as capital in the banking sector. I remember reading it twice, struck by something unusual: here was a senior executive in Zimbabwe's corporate world writing not about market share or profit margins, but about *people*. About trust as dividend and about connection as currency.

That article led me to seek her out. Our first conversation stretched well beyond its scheduled time, ranging from Shona proverbs to marketplace dynamics, from her childhood in Mkoba township to the complexities of leading with integrity in high-pressure environments. I left that conversation knowing I had encountered someone rare, a leader whose success had not hardened her, whose seniority had not distanced her from humanity.

Since then, I have had the privilege of observing Betty in various contexts. I have watched her navigate corporate spaces with both competence and compassion. I have seen her speak at events where her presence commands respect, yet her humility disarms. I have heard stories from her colleagues about her leadership style, one that values presence over performance, that sponsors rather than competes, that builds rather than hoards.

What makes this book powerful is not just what Betty says, but *who* she is. I have come to know her as someone who lives what she preaches. The relational wealth she writes about is not theory; it is practice. She truly does remember the names of cleaners and security guards. She truly does sponsor younger professionals without expecting credit. She truly does lead with a gentleness that is often mistaken for softness, until you realize how much strength it takes to remain tender in harsh environments.

This book is deeply African, and I say that with pride. In a world fragmenting under the weight of hyper-individualism, Betty offers us *Ubuntu*, the ancient wisdom that declares "I am because we are." She reminds us that the survival strategies of her childhood, community over isolation, sharing over hoarding, belonging over status, are not nostalgic relics. They are solutions for a world desperately seeking reconnection.

What you will find in these pages is an invitation to count your wealth differently. Betty introduces us to what she calls "the human balance sheet", a framework for auditing not just our financial accounts, but our relational ones. Where are we making deposits of trust, presence, kindness? Where are we only withdrawing? Where have we allowed proximity to substitute for intentionality? Where have we confused success with accumulation rather than multiplication?

This book is for many readers. It is for corporate leaders exhausted by transactional relationships and hungry for deeper connection.

It is for young professionals navigating workplaces where politics can overshadow integrity. It is for families trying to stay bonded in an era that prizes independence over interdependence. It is for anyone who suspects that our obsession with individual success is impoverishing us all. It is for the African diaspora reclaiming Indigenous wisdom in contemporary contexts. It is for every person who has achieved what the world calls success, yet felt a hollow echo where fulfilment should be.

But perhaps most importantly, this book is for anyone who has felt invisible, Betty resonates with you. The woman balancing career and caregiving. The junior employee whose contributions go unnoticed. The faithful partner whose daily deposits seem taken for granted. The immigrant maintaining transnational family obligations. The leader who projects strength while nursing private wounds. Betty resonates with you because she has been you.

As you read, you will encounter Betty's faith woven throughout. It is not preachy or performative; it is foundational. Her Christian conviction shapes how she defines success, how she practices forgiveness, how she understands legacy, and how she survived seasons that could have broken her. Whether you share her faith or not, you will recognize the authenticity of someone whose beliefs are not compartmentalized but integrated into every dimension of life.

You will also encounter Shona proverbs, compact wisdom from Betty's cultural heritage. These proverbs are not decorative; they are instructive. They contain strategies for survival, blueprints for community, frameworks for flourishing. Betty offers them not as quaint folklore, but as tested truth that has sustained people through centuries of challenge.

Some may find Betty's vulnerability uncomfortable. She does not present herself as having arrived, as having mastered all she teaches. She admits uncertainty, acknowledges ongoing growth, and names her own failures. But this is precisely what makes her trustworthy. We have enough gurus claiming perfection. We need more guides admitting struggle while still pointing toward truth.

If you are reading this book seeking formulas, you may be disappointed. Betty offers no five-step programs or guaranteed outcomes. What she offers is more valuable: a way of *seeing*. A lens through which relationships become not extras but essentials, not soft concerns but strategic capital, not peripheral but foundational to everything that matters.

My hope is that you will read slowly. That you will pause when a story resonates, or a proverb pierces. That you will do the audits Betty suggests, of your relational portfolios, your human balance sheets, and your legacy accounts. That you will ask yourself the questions she poses: Who are my master keys? Who am I becoming a master key for? What am I depositing in my closest relationships? Where am I overdrawn? What will remain when titles and positions fade?

Most importantly, my hope is that this book will change not just how you think about relationships, but how you practice them. That you will move from transaction to investment. From proximity to presence. From assumption to intention. From accumulation to multiplication.

Betty often quotes the proverb: "*Munhu munhu nekuda kwevanhu*", a person is a person because of other people. This book is her gift of that wisdom to a world that desperately needs reminding. At the end of our lives, the only wealth that truly matters is the love we gave, the trust we built, the lives we touched, the legacy we left in relationships that endure.

Welcome to Betty Murambadoro's world. May her journey illuminate yours.

Dr. Vongai Nyahunzvi
Managing Partner, Equinexus Partners

Preface

This book began as a collection of articles I wrote for the *Financial Gazette*. At the time, I simply wanted to share insights from my career in banking and leadership, lessons about people, trust, and navigating relationships in professional spaces. But as I revisited those writings, I realised they were pieces of a much larger story.

The real story was not about numbers, markets, or transactions; it was about relationships. Every achievement, every lesson, every scar in my life could be traced back to the wealth of people around me, family, neighbours, mentors, colleagues, marketplace participants, even strangers whose kindness or courage left a mark. I realised that what I was really writing all along was not about finance, but about the capital of connection.

I grew up in Mkoba, a township where resources were scarce, but community was abundant. I saw neighbours share food when cupboards were empty. I saw families raise children together. I learned that survival was not about what you had in your hand, but who you had by your side. Those early lessons shaped me far more than I knew at the time. Later, in banking and the marketplace, I discovered that the same principle applied: trust and connection were more valuable than numbers on a page.

Over the years, relationships have been both my greatest joy and my deepest pain. They have lifted me to heights I could not have reached alone. They have wounded me in ways that left scars. They have taught me empathy, resilience, humility, and wisdom. They have also revealed to me that the true measure of wealth is not what we accumulate, but what we invest in one another.

This book is my attempt to capture that truth. It is not a textbook, though you will find principles. It is not simply a memoir, though you will hear my story. It is not a leadership manual, though leaders may find guidance here. It is all of these and more, because relationships touch every part of life.

My hope is that as you read, you will see yourself in these pages. Perhaps you will recall a neighbour who shaped you, a mentor who believed in you, a colleague who stood by you, or even a scar that taught you. I pray that these stories and reflections will invite you to count your wealth differently, not only in money or titles, but in love, trust, and connection.

I write as a banker, but also as a daughter, a mother, a friend, a leader, and most of all, as a human being still learning. My heart is not to give you perfect answers, but to share what I have lived: that relationships are not extras; they are essentials. They are the real accounts worth guarding, the real legacies worth leaving.

As you journey through these pages, I encourage you to pause and reflect. Take stock of your personal balance sheet, not just your finances, but also your friendships, family, and faith. Consider the investments you are making in what truly matters. For ultimately, the world's greatest wealth isn't found in banks or markets, but in the people we cherish, the trust we cultivate, and the lives we impact. This is relational wealth, the legacy I aspire to build, and the path I now invite you to share with me.

Betty Murambadoro

...>>>...

Prologue: The First Intercessor I Ever Knew

Before I learned the language of leadership, before I stood on any stage or wrote any words, I watched a woman bend her knees in prayer, my mother. She was the first intercessor I ever knew.

I didn't always understand her strength. As a child, I only saw the surface: meals prepared on time, uniforms ironed, tears wiped without fanfare. But beneath it all was a woman anchored in God. Her prayers weren't loud, but they were laced with fire. She carried burdens that would have broken others, and yet she did not break. She bent, in prayer, in humility, in fierce love, but she did not break.

There were nights I would hear her whispering in Shona, calling out names in the dark. She prayed for our protection, our futures, our healing. She prayed when money ran out, she prayed when peace seemed distant. She prayed when no one else saw. And in those whispered intercessions, she laid the foundation for everything I would later become.

My mother led without titles, she built without applause; she nurtured faith in an environment that often gave her little rest.

And through it all, she taught me that prayer is not weakness; it is strategy. It is survival, it is leadership. This book, in so many ways, is her legacy. The lessons I share, the insights I've gained, the healing I speak of, all have roots in the soil of her faithfulness.

She did not wear a crown, but she walked like a queen. She did not carry a mic, but her prayers echoed in heaven. She is the reason I know the power of a woman on her knees.

To my mother, thank you. For every whispered prayer. For every unspoken sacrifice. For every lesson taught not in words, but in the way you lived, this is for you. You were my first teacher, my first leader. The first intercessor I ever knew.

A Note on Shona Proverbs

Throughout this book, you will encounter Shona proverbs, compact wisdom passed down through generations of my Zimbabwean heritage. These proverbs are more than sayings; they are strategies for survival, blueprints for community, and maps for navigating relationships.

In Shona culture, proverbs are spoken in moments of teaching, conflict, celebration, and grief. Elders use them to guide the young, mothers whisper them to children, and communities invoke them to restore harmony. They carry the distilled wisdom of centuries.

I have translated each proverb as it appears, so you can absorb both the sound of my mother tongue and the meaning it carries. Some proverbs appear multiple times because their truths are foundational, worth repeating, worth remembering, worth carrying forward.

I invite you to let these proverbs speak not only as African wisdom, but as universal truth. Because while the language is Shona, the insights are human. And in a fractured world, we all need the reminders they offer: that we belong to one another, that relationships require investment, that survival is communal.

May these proverbs become companions on your own journey toward relational wealth.

CONTENTS

Introduction

We live in a world overflowing with information and innovation, but starving for connection. We are more "connected" than ever through gadgets, social media, and technology, yet loneliness has become a global epidemic. Trust in institutions is at a historic low. Families are fractured. Organisations rise and fall not only because of financial mismanagement, but also because of relational breakdowns. Nations themselves are torn apart by the erosion of trust between leaders and citizens.

In a world where many question the true nature of enduring wealth, we've long been told it's financial: accumulating assets and maximizing profit. However, I've observed marketplace participants with extensive portfolios who were impoverished in their relationships. They possessed money but lacked peace, wielded influence without trust, and achieved success with no one to share it. It became clear to me then that while money is important, it is not the ultimate measure.

Others told us the answer was systems and processes, build structures, perfect strategies, rely on efficiency, and yet, I have watched flawless systems collapse because trust was missing.

I have seen brilliant strategies fail because people would not work together. I have seen efficient organisations hollowed out by toxic cultures. Systems matter, but they are not sufficient. The real wealth, the capital that sustains when money fades and systems fail, is relational.

There is a Shona proverb: *"Munhu munhu nekuda kwevanhu."* A person is a person because of other people. This ancient truth is also a modern strategy. It is not only about survival in communities like Mkoba, where I grew up. It is about thriving in the global marketplace, in families, in organisations, in nations. Without relationships, nothing lasts. With them, even the impossible becomes possible.

This conviction has been shaped by my journey, from the township streets of Zimbabwe to the corridors of finance, from childhood scars to marketplace strategies, from grief to resilience. Along the way, I have discovered that relationships are not sentimental extras. They are the foundation of everything. They are assets that can be invested in, liabilities that can drain, and portfolios that must be stewarded.

That is why I have written this book. Not to add another voice to the overload of leadership manuals or self-help guides, but to offer a perspective I believe the world desperately needs: that relational wealth is the most enduring wealth we can build.

This book is divided into four parts:

- Part I: Roots of Relational Wealth, the early years, the family influences, the scars and seeds that shaped my heart for relationships.

- Part II: Banking on Relationships, lessons from the world of finance and leadership, where I discovered that trust and connection are the real assets in any portfolio.

- Part III: The Human Advantage, insights for today's world, where technology advances but empathy, trust, and belonging remain the competitive edge.

- Part IV: Legacy Accounts, reflections on what endures beyond us, and how to build accounts of love, trust, and connection that outlast our years.

Along the way, you will find stories from my own life, proverbs from my culture, lessons from my faith, and principles I hope you can apply in your own journey. Some will encourage you. Some may challenge you. All are written with one conviction: that relationships are the world's real capital. My hope is that this book does three things for you:

1. Helps you audit your own relational balance sheet to see where you are rich, where you may be in deficit, and where you can invest more wisely.

2. Encourages you to revalue what matters most, to shift your gaze from numbers and titles to people and trust.

3. Inspires you to build legacy accounts, to deposit love, wisdom, and kindness daily into relationships that will endure beyond you.

The world does not need more isolated stars; it needs constellations. It needs communities, families, leaders, neighbours, and nations who know that we rise together or we fall apart.

So I invite you to walk with me through these pages, to revisit your own roots. To reflect on your own scars. To rethink your own leadership. And above all, to rediscover the capital of connection that will carry us into the future. Because the future is not financial, technological, or political. The future is relational.

Part I: Roots of Relational Wealth

CHAPTER 1

The Making of a Relational Heart

I was born into a world where relationships were not optional, they were oxygen. In Mkoba, survival was not guaranteed by money in the bank or food in the cupboard. It was guaranteed by people, by neighbours who checked on each other, by families who carried each other's burdens, by children who belonged to the whole community, not just their parents.

In Mkoba, the houses were small, and the walls were thin. You could hear laughter from the neighbour's yard as easily as your own. Pots were often empty, yet somehow there was always enough. If one family had little, another would share. I remember the aroma of sadza drifting from a neighbour's kitchen when ours was bare. Without hesitation, someone would knock, and suddenly a single meal became enough for two families. That was my first education in relational wealth: that survival was never about how much you had, but about who you had beside you.

Of course, it was not only generosity that shaped me, there were shadows, too. My childhood was marked by the quiet strength of my mother and the pain of watching her endure more than she should have. Behind closed doors, I saw how love can wound as well as heal, how words can cut deeper than knives, how pain leaves scars not just on bodies but on children's hearts. I learned too young that relationships are powerful; they can destroy, or they can sustain. That truth has never left me.

My mother was the first relational leader I ever knew. She had very little in terms of material wealth, but she had a deep well of resilience and faith. I would often hear her praying in the night, her whispered words filling the silence with hope. She prayed for her children, for protection, for a better tomorrow. Her prayers did not flow from circumstances, but from faith as her only anchor. Watching her taught me that leadership begins not with commanding others, but with carrying them in your heart.

In the streets of Mkoba, I found my place of belonging. Friendships were fragile but formative. I remember moments of exclusion, where I stood at the edges of games, longing to be invited in. Those moments hurt more than I can explain. As a child, I could not articulate it, but I felt the truth: rejection leaves a mark. It tells you a story about yourself, and if you are not careful, you begin to believe it. But inclusion heals. Every time a friend pulled me into the circle, every time someone said, "Come, play with us," I felt whole again. Those early wounds and healings etched into me a sensitivity to belonging that I carry to this day.

There is a Shona proverb: *"Ukama igasva hunozadziswa nekudya."*

Relationships are incomplete until they are nourished. In Mkoba, that was not just a saying; it was a lived reality. Relationships were nourished through shared meals, visits, and the caring of one another's children. That proverb shaped me long before I understood its depth. It taught me that relationships must be fed, not assumed. Left unattended, they wither; nurtured, they flourish.

School added another layer. It was there that I began to realise that relationships extend beyond family and neighbours; they are the currency of every community. Teachers could make or break you with a word. Friends could lift you or isolate you. Success was not just about grades, but about the networks you formed, the trust you earned, and the alliances you built. Looking back, I can see that even in the classroom, I was already learning the truth I would one day articulate in the marketplace: relationships are capital.

My faith was another thread running through those years. Sunday mornings were filled with hymns, with voices lifted in worship, with sermons about love, forgiveness, and endurance. I may not have understood all the theology as a child, but I absorbed both the atmosphere and the conviction that we are bound to one another, that our lives are not our own, that love is the greatest commandment.

That conviction became my compass, even when life later pulled me into places where faith was unfashionable.

When I look back now, I see clearly how these early experiences formed the bedrock of my relational heart. Poverty taught me the value of generosity. Harsh discipline taught me the importance of empathy. Exclusion taught me the necessity of belonging. Faith taught me the power of love. Together, they shaped a worldview in which relationships are not optional extras, but the very core of survival, success, and legacy.

I often say that the greatest wealth is not found in accounts or assets, but in people. That truth did not come to me in a bank; it came to me in Mkoba. It came to me in the resilience of my mother, the open door of Aunt Cathy, the kindness of neighbours, the pain of exclusion, the healing of friendship, and the whispered prayers at night. These were my first deposits in the account of relational wealth.

The most incredible lesson from my childhood is that even the most fractured stories can be redeemed through relationships. My relationship with my father grew deeper through years of intentional engagement and prayer, not by erasing the past, but by allowing love to inscribe a new chapter. This challenging journey, detailed later in the book, began with the understanding that relationships, despite their fragility, possess the power of reconstruction.

I begin this book not in the marketplace, but in Mkoba. This is because leadership, strategy, and even wealth are built on a deeper foundation: the soil of relationships. Before we discuss portfolios and politics, we must acknowledge the mothers who pray, the neighbors who share, the aunts who welcome, and the children who long to belong. This is the making of a relational heart, and it is where my story begins.

CHAPTER 2

Love, Loss, and the Lessons from Home

Home is supposed to be a place of safety, a place where laughter echoes in the walls, where love steadies your steps, where belonging wraps you like a blanket at night. For me, home was both that and something else. It was love and loss living side by side. It was resilience and fracture, prayers and pain. It was the school where I learned my earliest lessons about the power and fragility of relationships.

My mother was the heartbeat of our home. She carried burdens no woman should have to bear, yet she did so with grace. I watched her face battles no one should face, battles that left scars not visible to the eye but etched into her spirit. Harsh discipline was a shadow that visited our home too often, and as a child, I struggled to make sense of it. I wanted to believe that love always nurtures, always protects. Instead, I learned too young that love can wound.

And yet, my mother also taught me something else. She taught me that pain does not have to define you. Even in the shadows, she chose dignity; she chose prayer. I can still hear her whispering in the dark: prayers for protection, for provision, for peace. Her prayers were like a shield over us, a way of saying to God what she could not always say to others. Watching her, I learned that faith is not naïve; it is defiant. It is choosing hope when circumstances offer none.

Back then, my father was a complex man. To see him only as an extensive disciplinarian or tough negotiator in child discipline would be unfair, because he was also part of my becoming. He provided in the ways he knew how. He worked hard. He was not only tough; he had moments of tenderness, flashes of care. But the truth is, his anger often spoke louder than his love. As a little girl, I longed for a father whose gentleness could match my mother's resilience. That longing left its mark on me.

As I grew older, I began to see my parents not as heroes or villains, but as humans, humans shaped by their own scars, their own histories, their own battles. That realisation planted the first seed of empathy in me and made forgiveness seem possible, at least in theory. In practice, however, reconciliation with my father was neither quick nor simple. It was a long, painful, and imperfect journey marked by prayer, confusion, and hard-won boundaries. I often found myself torn between the desire to honour my father and the need to protect myself from further hurt.

Over the years that followed, I learned that forgiveness is not a straight line. There were seasons when I kept my distance from my father to safeguard my own heart. I had to learn that forgiving him did not mean allowing him to hurt me again. With time and the guidance of wise mentors, I set boundaries, an act of self-respect that my mother's quiet dignity had always taught me. Still, I prayed continually for him and for our fractured relationship. On some days, I prayed with a hopeful heart, believing that God could soften what was hardened. On other days, I prayed through clenched teeth, asking God to take away the anger and bitterness I sometimes felt. Each tentative step toward reconciliation carried an emotional cost; each tentative step also carried a seed of healing.

For many years, my father resisted every invitation to truly mend our relationship. He bristled at the idea of therapy or counseling, perhaps out of pride or out of fear of facing the past. If I even suggested that we seek outside help or talk about what happened, he would dismiss it outright. "I don't need to talk to strangers about my family," he once snapped when I raised the idea of counseling. In his mind, the past was something to be left alone, sealed off by silence. There were times I wondered if we would ever move beyond the polite, careful conversations on holidays into genuine healing.

Many nights, I felt defeated, asking myself if continued effort was worth the pain of repeated rebuffs.

My father went through a series of biblical teachings and unpacking elements of his past, thanks to the two pastors based in Harare, who graciously made trips to Gweru and also mentored him telephonically. My father eventually got baptized under the counsel of these two pastors.

Looking back now, I see that my heart for relationships was forged right there, in the tension of love and loss, of fracture and faith. I learned that relationships matter because they shape us at the deepest level. They can scar us, yes, but they can also heal us. They can break us, but they can also build us. They can silence us, but they can also give us a voice. The very same home that wounded me also equipped me with compassion and resilience.

As I entered adulthood, I carried both the scars and the strength of my home. The scars gave me empathy, and the strength gave me resilience. Together, they made me a woman determined to value relationships, to nurture them and to protect them. I could not always protect my mother from harm, but I could build a life where others felt seen and safe. That became my silent vow: to create spaces of love and safety wherever I could, in honour of what my mother taught me and what my father and I eventually reclaimed.

So when I speak now about relational wealth, I am not speaking from theory. I am speaking from survival, from nights of whispered prayers and days of hard-won forgiveness. I speak from meals shared by generous neighbours when our own kitchen was empty. I speak from reconciliations that seemed impossible but became real in time. I speak from the lessons of love and loss that made me who I am.

This is the paradox of home: it broke me, and it built me. It gave me wounds, and it gave me wisdom. It left me longing, and it left me loved. And all of it, every moment of pain, every glimpse of grace, became part of the making of my relational heart.

Proverbs That Shaped Me

Long before I read leadership books or sat in the marketplace, my teachers were the elders in my community and the words they spoke in proverbs. Shona proverbs are more than sayings. They are condensed wisdom, short enough to be remembered but deep enough to guide a lifetime. As a child, I did not always understand them, but they lingered. They were repeated in kitchens, whispered in moments of conflict, thrown at us when we disobeyed, or used to explain why things happened the way they did. Over time, they seeped into me. Looking back now, I realise they were shaping my understanding of relationships before I even had language for "relational wealth."

One of the first I remember hearing was: "*Ukama igasva hunozadziswa nekudya.*" Relationships are incomplete until they are nourished. As a little girl, I thought this was only about food. And in Mkoba, it made sense:

sharing a plate of *sadza* was often the way bonds were confirmed. But as I grew older, I understood its wider meaning. Relationships must be fed, they do not survive on words alone.

They need time, attention, forgiveness, and generosity. I saw it in my neighbours, who made space for others at their tables. I saw it in my aunt, who offered food as a way of saying, "You belong here." I carry that truth into leadership now: if you do not nourish the relationships around you, they will wither, no matter how much strategy or talent you have.

Another proverb I heard often was: "*Rume rimwe harikombi churu.*" One man alone cannot surround an anthill. I witnessed it early in the way neighbours came together to solve problems, fetching water when pipes burst, caring for children when parents were away, pulling together money for funerals. It was never one person's effort. Survival was communal. Later, in my career, I saw the same truth in teams. No single genius is enough, no leader succeeds alone, and greatness is always collective. That proverb became a quiet strategy in my leadership: build alliances, invest in teams, never walk alone.

There was also: "*Chakafukidza dzimba matenga.*" The roof covers the secrets of homes. To me, then, it meant that what happened in families was often hidden. I knew it all too well from my own home, where strictness left scars behind closed doors. At the time, it felt like a curse. It meant suffering carried in silence. But as I grew, I also saw another layer. The proverb reminded me not to judge too quickly.

Every home carries secrets, every person carries burdens unseen. That realisation gave me empathy. It made me more patient with colleagues, more compassionate with strangers, and more forgiving with those who hurt me. Because behind every polished face, there may be hidden wounds.

There were lighter ones too. "*Chitsva chiri murutsoka.*" What is new is found in your own footsteps. My mother used to say this when she encouraged me to go out, to learn, to walk my path. It was a reminder that growth does not come from waiting, but from moving. Today, I hear it as a call to courage: if you want to discover new things, you must take the step yourself. No one else can walk your journey for you.

And there was: "*Rudo runobereka vamwe.*" Love multiplies others. This one is simple but incredible. It was lived in the way communities raised children together, in the way a single act of kindness sparked more kindness. I see it now in mentoring, in sponsorship, in the way one leader's encouragement can ripple through generations. Love multiplies. It expands influence far beyond what titles or money can do.

Growing up, I sometimes rolled my eyes at these proverbs. They seemed old-fashioned, spoken by elders who wanted to remind us of rules. But now, I see they were forming a worldview. They were teaching me that relationships matter more than possessions, that community is stronger than isolation, that empathy is wiser than judgment, that love multiplies wealth in ways money never can.

Having faith deepened this perspective. Many of the proverbs echoed Scripture: gentleness building rather than destroying, love multiplying, the body needing all its parts. They connected African wisdom with biblical truth, giving me a double inheritance of relational guidance.

Looking back, I am grateful for the elders who spoke these words into my life. They probably did not think of themselves as teachers of leadership or strategy. They were simply passing down survival wisdom. But those words became seeds. Seeds that sprouted in the marketplace, in friendships, in grief, in faith. Seeds that shaped the way I understand the world.

When I speak now about relational wealth, I am not only drawing from my career. I am drawing from these proverbs. They taught me that relationships need nurturing, that no one thrives alone, that every person carries hidden struggles, that gentleness builds more than harshness, that courage requires walking, that love multiplies. This wisdom was not written in textbooks. It was written in the cadence of my people's speech, carried across generations, etched into my childhood.

So when people ask me how I came to believe so strongly in the power of relationships, I often smile. Because the truth is, the seeds were planted long ago, in Mkoba, in my home, in the words of elders. My relational heart was being shaped not only by experience but by proverbs that carried the distilled wisdom of countless lives before me.

These proverbs are more than cultural artefacts. They are strategies for survival, blueprints for leadership, guides for legacy. And they remind me that the wealth I speak of in this book is not new. It is ancient wisdom, lived and proven, waiting for us to rediscover it.

CHAPTER 4

The School of Belonging

Every child longs to belong. We may not have words for it when we are small, but our hearts know it. We know it in the way we watch others playing and hope to be invited. We feel it when we carry the sting of rejection long after others have forgotten. Belonging is not a luxury. It is a need as basic as food and shelter. I learned that lesson early.

Mkoba was a place where children played freely. We made toys out of wire, balls out of plastic bags, games out of the dust and our imaginations. The streets were alive with laughter and arguments, with children racing and chanting. It should have been paradise for any child, but even there, belonging was not guaranteed. There were times when I stood at the edge of a game, waiting for someone to call my name. Sometimes they did, and my heart soared. Sometimes they didn't, and my heart sank.

The sting of exclusion is sharp. I still remember the burn in my chest when I was told, "Not you today," or when I saw friends walk away without me.

At that age, you cannot reason with yourself. You cannot say, "They are only children, it doesn't matter." It does matter; it carves something into you. It tells you a story about your worth. And if you are not careful, that story follows you into adulthood.

But there were also moments of belonging, and those moments healed as much as rejection hurt. The joy of belonging is as powerful as the pain of exclusion. Both leave marks. Both become teachers.

I realise now that belonging was one of my first currencies of relational wealth. It was traded in playgrounds and classrooms, in invitations and exclusions. It was as valuable to me then as any bank account would later be. In many ways, it still is.

There is a Shona proverb: "*Musha mukadzi.*" A home is built by a woman. I think often of my mother when I hear that, but I also think of the women and girls around me who created belonging. My mother created belonging with her prayers and presence. My aunt created it with her open door. My friends created it with invitations into their circles. Women carried the gift of making spaces feel like home. I learned from them that belonging is not accidental; it is created.

School was another place where belonging was tested. Classrooms were filled with invisible hierarchies. Who sat where, who was chosen for groups, who was praised by teachers, all of it communicated who belonged and who did not. I remember longing for affirmation from teachers, not only for my work but for myself. When I received it, it fuelled me. When I didn't, I wrestled with doubt. School taught me that belonging is not only social; it is institutional. Systems can either include or exclude, and those choices shape destinies.

My faith also played a role. Church was a place of belonging for me. Even when home felt fractured, I found community in worship, in youth groups, in Scripture that reminded me that I was seen and loved by God. I clung to verses that spoke of being chosen, of being adopted, of being part of a family larger than blood. Those truths were lifelines. They told me a different story than the one exclusion whispered. They said, "You are beloved. You belong."

As I grew older, I saw how the patterns of childhood carried into adulthood. Adults still long to be included. We still feel the sting of rejection and the joy of belonging. Only the playgrounds change, instead of games, we compete for seats at tables, for invitations to rooms of influence, for recognition in marketplaces. The desire is the same, and the stakes are higher.

In my career, I saw how exclusion could crush confidence and how belonging could unlock potential. A leader's words of affirmation could change the trajectory of someone's career. A colleague's silence could erode it. I never forgot my childhood lessons. They made me determined to be a leader who created belonging, not exclusion.

There is another proverb that says, "*Chara chimwe hachitswanyi inda.*" One finger alone cannot crush a louse. Belonging is about recognising that we need each other. No one thrives alone. Isolation may feel safe, but it is not sustainable. Belonging is strength. It multiplies courage, it fuels resilience, it creates spaces where people can bring their whole selves.

Looking back, I see my childhood as a school of belonging. It was not always gentle. It taught me through wounds as well as gifts. But it gave me a sensitivity I now consider one of my greatest strengths. I notice who is left out. I notice who is silent. I notice who sits at the edge of the circle. And I remember that little girl in Mkoba, longing for an invitation. That memory keeps me soft. It reminds me to stretch out my hand, to make space, to say, "Come join us."

Faith confirms this calling. The Gospel itself is a story of belonging restored, of a God who gathers the excluded, who welcomes the lost, who makes strangers into family. If this is God's heart, then it must be mine too.

Belonging, I now see, is not just a childhood longing. It is the foundation of relational wealth. Without it, relationships are shallow and transactional. With it, they are deep and enduring. Belonging is what makes us human.

So when I speak today about the importance of relationships, I am speaking from the school of belonging. A school that taught me through games in dusty streets, through tears of rejection, through laughter of inclusion, and through prayers of faith. A school that continues to shape how I lead, how I love, how I live. Because in the end, the richest account any of us can carry is the sense that we are seen, valued, and included and that we belong.

CHAPTER 5

Faith as Anchor

When I think about what has carried me through life, through the joys and the storms, the betrayals and the breakthroughs, one word comes to mind: faith. Not faith as a Sunday ritual, not faith as a label, but faith as an anchor. The kind of faith that steadies you when everything else feels uncertain. The kind of faith that whispers hope in the dark and reminds you that you are never truly alone.

My first encounters with faith came not from books or sermons but from my mother's prayers. I can still hear her voice in the quiet of the night, low and insistent, rising above the silence of our small home. Sometimes she prayed for protection, sometimes for provision, sometimes simply for strength to make it through another day. Those prayers were more than words. They were survival. They were her way of lifting burdens too heavy for her shoulders and placing them into God's hands.

As a child, I did not always understand the depth of her faith, but I absorbed its rhythm. I absorbed the conviction that there is a God who sees, who cares, who is present even in the hardest moments. Watching my mother taught me that faith is not about denying pain. It is about refusing to let pain have the last word.

Church was another anchor. Sunday mornings were an escape from the heaviness of home. They were filled with hymns that lifted my spirit, Scripture that spoke of love and redemption, and community that made me feel seen. In church, I was not the child of a fractured home. I was a child of God, beloved and chosen. That truth wrapped around me like a cloak, giving me a sense of identity I desperately needed.

There is a Shona proverb: "*Mwari ane munhu wake.*" God has His own person. It was a way of reminding us that God watches over His people, that no one is forgotten. I clung to that saying, especially in moments when life felt unfair. It reassured me that even when I felt unseen by people, I was not unseen by God.

My faith also gave me language for belonging. The Gospel spoke of adoption into God's family, of being chosen, of being loved unconditionally. Those truths countered the lies exclusion tried to tell me. They reminded me that my worth was not negotiable, not dependent on others' acceptance. I belonged, not because of what I achieved, but because of who I was in God's eyes. That foundation became crucial later in life, when rejection or betrayal threatened to shake me.

As I entered adulthood and stepped into the professional world, faith continued to be my anchor. Banking is not an industry known for gentleness or grace. It is driven by numbers, competition, and pressure. In that environment, it would have been easy to lose myself, to compromise my values, to let ambition overshadow integrity. But faith held me steady. It reminded me that success without integrity is failure. It reminded me that my worth was not tied to my performance, but to my identity in God.

There were moments when I faced difficult decisions, when doing the right thing meant losing opportunities. In those moments, I leaned on faith. I prayed for wisdom, for courage, for discernment. Often, the path of integrity was the harder one, but it was the one I could live with. Faith became my compass, pointing me back to truth when the world offered shortcuts.

Faith also carried me through grief. Losing loved ones felt unbearable, but faith reminded me that death is not the end. I found comfort in Scriptures that spoke of eternal life, of God wiping away every tear, of a hope that cannot be destroyed. Grief still hurt, but faith gave it context. It gave me permission to mourn and yet to hope. It gave me the strength to comfort others, because I had been comforted myself.

I often think of the story in the Bible where Jesus calms the storm. The disciples are terrified, convinced they are about to drown, while Jesus sleeps peacefully in the boat. When they wake Him, He calms the wind and the waves with a word. That story resonates deeply with me. Life has given me storms, storms at home, storms at the marketplace, storms in my heart. But again and again, faith has been my anchor.

Even when the storm raged, I knew there was a presence greater than the waves. In leadership, faith gave me a different lens. It taught me to see people not just as employees or marketplace participants, but as human beings made in the image of God. It taught me to value dignity over profit, compassion over efficiency, relationships over transactions. Those were not always popular priorities, but they were the ones that gave my leadership meaning.

There is another Shona proverb that says, "*Kusvika kureba hakusi kusvikira Mwari.*" Reaching far is not reaching God. It reminds me that no matter how successful we become, we are never beyond God's reach. Faith humbled me in my achievements and steadied me in my failures. It kept me from being intoxicated by success or crushed by disappointment.

Of course, faith was not always easy. There were seasons of doubt, times when prayers seemed unanswered, times when God felt distant. But even then, faith was a thread that held me. Sometimes thin, sometimes frayed, but always present. And looking back, I see that God was there even when I could not feel Him.

Faith also shaped my vision for legacy. I do not want to be remembered only for my career or accomplishments. I want to be remembered for my love, my integrity, my compassion. And those qualities flow from faith. They are the fruits of the anchor that has held me all these years.

When I think of faith as an anchor, I picture my mother on her knees, whispering prayers into the night. I picture hymns rising in a small township church. I picture myself in the marketplace, praying silently for wisdom before speaking. I picture tears on my face, and the quiet assurance that God is near. That is faith. Not always dramatic, not always visible, but steady, strong, enduring.

And so, as I write this book about relationships, I cannot separate them from faith. For me, the two are intertwined. Faith is the foundation that shapes how I relate to others, how I lead, how I forgive, and how I hope. It is the anchor that steadies my relational heart. Because at the end of the day, storms will come. People will disappoint. Systems will fail. But faith remains. And it is that faith, lived, tested, and proven, that has carried me from Mkoba to the marketplace, from scars to strategies, from survival to legacy.

CHAPTER 6

Scars That Became Seeds

Scars tell stories, they are proof that pain has passed through us, that we were wounded but survived. For years, I thought of my scars as things to hide. They felt like signs of weakness, marks of shame. I wanted to cover them, to pretend they did not exist. But life has taught me something different: scars can become seeds. They can grow into wisdom, empathy, and purpose if we choose to let them.

My first scars were from home. The conflicts, the strict discipline, the silence afterwards, all of it etched something into me. As a child, I thought those experiences diminished me. I thought they made me less. But later, I realised they gave me a unique sensitivity. Because I knew what it felt like to see someone suffer, I noticed pain in others more quickly. Because I knew the ache of brokenness, I cherished belonging more deeply. Those scars became seeds of empathy and of my conviction that relationships must be places of safety, not harm.

There is a Shona proverb: "*Anorohwa nomunhu haaregi kutaura*." The one who is struck does not stop speaking. Pain does not silence truth. If anything, it amplifies it. My scars gave me a voice. They gave me courage to say, "This is not how relationships should be." They pushed me to build a life where kindness, not cruelty, was the foundation. They gave me the strength to say to others: you are not defined by your pain.

School added its own scars. The sting of exclusion, the ache of being left out, the silent question of whether I mattered. Those moments pierced me in ways that lingered far beyond childhood. But they also became seeds. They grew into a deep awareness of belonging, into the instinct to notice who is left on the margins. They made me the kind of leader who looks for the person at the edge of the circle, who asks the quiet one in the room to speak, who insists on pulling people in. Exclusion scarred me, but it also seeded in me a lifelong calling to create belonging.

Later, in my career, more scars came. Betrayals in the marketplace. Politics that undermined my work. Colleagues who shut doors in my face. Those wounds cut deep. For a while, they left me questioning my worth. But over time, they cultivated discernment. I learned not to trust every smile. I learned to look for substance, not performance. I learned the value of true allies and the danger of counterfeit ones. Those scars became a strategy, not to grow bitter, but to grow wise.

Grief left its marks, too. Losing loved ones, standing at gravesides, watching futures disappear, these scars were some of the heaviest. They could have hardened me, made me bitter, made me close my heart. Instead, they softened me. They seeded compassion.

They reminded me that behind every professional title, behind every polished face, there may be hidden sorrow. They taught me to lead with gentleness, to extend grace, to value presence over performance.

Faith was the soil where these seeds could grow. Without faith, I might have buried my scars in bitterness. With faith, I could see them differently. I thought often of Jesus after the resurrection, when He still bore scars in His hands. His scars were not erased, but they were redeemed. They were no longer wounds; they were testimonies. That truth gave me courage to embrace my own scars, not as things to hide, but as reminders of survival, as seeds of purpose.

One of the most important lessons I learned is that scars connect us. People may admire your strengths, but they relate to your scars. When I began to share my struggles, carefully, honestly, I saw others lean in. My vulnerability gave them permission to be real, too. Trust deepened in those moments. Teams grew stronger. Friendships became more authentic. Scars, when shared wisely, become bridges.

Looking back, I can trace how each scar became a seed:

- Harsh discipline at home → seed of empathy and desire for safe relationships.
- Exclusion at school → seed of sensitivity to belonging.
- Betrayals in the marketplace → seed of discernment and integrity.
- Grief → seed of compassion and presence.

Together, these seeds grew into my relational heart. They shaped the way I see leadership, the way I value people, and the way I define wealth. Without them, I might have pursued only titles and money. With them, I discovered that the greatest capital is trust, empathy, and love.

There is another proverb: "*Chitsva chiri murutsoka.*" What is new is found in your own footsteps. Each scar marked a step I would not have chosen, but each step led me to new wisdom. Painful as they were, those footsteps carried seeds I could not have found otherwise.

When I mentor others now, I often tell them: do not despise your scars. They are not signs of failure. They are proof of survival. And if you choose to plant them, they can grow into strength you never imagined. So yes, my life has scars. They are part of my story. But they are also my seeds. Seeds that grew into resilience. Seeds that grew into empathy. Seeds that grew into the conviction that relationships are not just soft extras, but the true wealth of our lives. Because in the end, it is not the absence of scars that makes us strong. It is the seeds we grow from them.

CHAPTER 7

Betrayals of the Heart, Trust, Forgiveness, and Healing

Some wounds are invisible but cut the deepest. They don't leave bruises you can point to or bandage with gauze. They live under your skin, in your chest, in your breath, in the fragile way your heart beats after it's been broken by someone you trusted most. This is the terrain of betrayal. And nothing prepares you for it.

There was a time in my life when someone I loved deeply, betrayed me. It wasn't a dramatic moment; it unfolded slowly, painfully. A series of small choices, quiet omissions, and the sudden realisation that love had not guarded me the way I thought it would. I remember feeling hollow, like the floor had fallen out from under me. I would sit in the dark, praying, not for vengeance or answers, but simply to breathe without crying.

"Why me, Lord?" I whispered more than once. "How could someone I opened my life to choose dishonesty over truth? Silence over vulnerability?" Betrayal is a thief. It doesn't just take away your trust in the other person; it steals your trust in yourself, too. I began to question my discernment, my worth, my instincts. I stopped trusting my own ability to see clearly, and in doing so, I began to guard my heart too tightly. I wore strength like armour, convincing the world that I had moved on, when inside, I was nursing wounds I didn't know how to name.

It would have been easier to turn bitter. To shut my heart entirely. But something inside me, faith, stubbornness, grace ,refused to let pain have the final word.

I started by seeking counsel. A wise mentor reminded me that wounds don't heal by ignoring them. They heal by cleaning them, dressing them, and tending to them over time. I went to therapy, reluctantly at first, but gradually I found a safe space to weep, to speak, to confront. I was reminded that forgiveness was not a gift to the one who hurt me; it was a gift to myself. Holding on to bitterness was like drinking poison and hoping the other person would suffer. I had to release it, not because they deserved peace, but because I did.

Forgiveness didn't come all at once. It came in layers, some as thin as silk, others as thick as iron. Some days I felt free, other days I felt the weight again. But with time, and honesty, and the unfailing grace of God, I began to mend.

There's a Japanese art form called *kintsugi*, the mending of broken pottery with gold. The cracks are not hidden; they are highlighted, made beautiful. That's how I see my heart now. It is not as pristine as it once was, but it is stronger. And in its cracks, grace shines.

Eventually, I could look at the person who betrayed me without flinching. I don't pretend nothing happened. I don't gloss over the cost. But I can say truthfully: I no longer carry the pain as a weapon. I carry it as wisdom. I carry it as a quiet reminder of the kind of woman I've become, one who has bled and healed, broken and rebuilt.

Trust, once broken, is like a bank account in overdraft. It takes time, repentance, and repeated deposits of honesty to rebuild. Whether that trust is ever fully restored or not, the process of healing is not wasted. It strengthens you, clarifies your boundaries, and sharpens your discernment.

Even leaders get betrayed. Even strong women cry. And what defines us is not the betrayal itself, but how we rise from it. I chose to rise, not with a closed heart, but with a wise one. I chose to love again, not recklessly, but courageously.

There is a proverb I hold onto: "Broken trust can be rebuilt with truth and time." And in Scripture, the story of Joseph reminds me: sometimes those closest to us will sell us out, and yet God can still lift us up. So no, I am not defined by betrayal. I am defined by resilience. By grace. By the decision to keep my heart open, not because it hasn't been hurt, but because it has, and it still beats, and that, too, is relational wealth.

CHAPTER 8

The Burden of Care, Love, Sacrifice, and Setting Boundaries

It was a Saturday morning in March of 2023, when I found myself once again on the long road to Gweru. The car hummed beneath me, and the sky was still heavy with sleep. I was going to care for my father again. And I loved him. I truly did. But love, I've learned, does not cancel out weariness. As the miles stretched ahead of me, so did the ache in my body, and in my heart.

He doesn't always remember the sacrifices. Some days, he forgets my name. Other days, he remembers only fragments of who I am, confusing me with a cousin or a childhood friend. And yet, I keep coming back. I feed him, wash his clothes, pray over him, and sit by his side even when he stares blankly past me. This is love, I tell myself. But some days, love feels like a weight I am not sure I can keep carrying.

As a family, I fought hard to get us to have honest conversations of what really transpired and work on our own healing.

We are in a good place as far as authentic conversations are concerned. We have found ways of facing the past together. There is a lot of collaboration we are going through.

That moment taught me the necessity of boundaries. I began to designate time for myself, one weekend a month that was just mine. I scheduled my own appointments, went away for spa days, rested, or simply stayed home in silence. And what surprised me most was that these moments of pause made me a better daughter. I showed up in Gweru less irritable, more present.

At first, I felt guilty. Our culture teaches us to honour our parents, to sacrifice endlessly. And I believe in honour. But honour must not come at the cost of self-destruction. Setting boundaries, I realised, was not dishonour, it was wisdom. It was choosing sustainability over martyrdom.

There's a Shona proverb that says, "*Ganda rembeva haridyiwi rimwe.*" One person cannot eat the entire mouse skin. Some tasks, some burdens, must be shared. And if they are not, we must at least allow ourselves the grace to rest.

Through this journey, I discovered new depths of compassion, not just for my father, but for caregivers everywhere. For the quiet women and men carrying their families, their parents, their communities on their backs. I understand now that love is not proven by how much we give until we collapse. Love is also shown in how well we care for ourselves so we can continue to show up for others.

This season also unearthed old tensions with my siblings, resentments, misunderstandings, and long-held grievances.

But with honest conversation and time, we began to heal, if only in small ways. A brother flew in for a visit. A sister sent money regularly. Others began to check in more consistently. It wasn't perfect, but it was progress.

To every caregiver reading this: your love is sacred. Your sacrifice is seen. But you, too, are valuable. You matter. Don't be afraid to protect your peace. Don't wait until you're broken to ask for help. Rest is holy. Boundaries are biblical. And joy, even in caregiving, is possible when we are not running on empty.

Relational wealth includes the relationship we have with ourselves. And in caring for my father, I learned to care for me, too.

CHAPTER 9

Entitlement vs. Gratitude, Reclaiming Respect in Relationships

There's a quiet erosion that happens when love and generosity are met not with appreciation, but with expectation. You don't notice it at first. You chalk it up to busy schedules, to cultural norms, to "they probably just forgot." But over time, entitlement reveals itself, and it stings.

There were other moments, too, where other close relational folks who always expected me to handle everything "because you're so good at it." A friend who would only call when she needed something, never to ask how I was doing. Slowly, I found myself avoiding calls, dreading text messages that began with "Hey, can I ask you for a favour?" And the truth is, I started to feel bitter. Me, the champion of relational wealth, the advocate for love, grace, and generosity, I was becoming resentful. That scared me.

A wise mentor saw through my silence and asked me gently, "When was the last time you felt valued instead of used?"

That question stopped me cold. I had to face a hard truth: I had taught people how to treat me. By never speaking up, by always saying yes, by acting like it didn't bother me, I had made entitlement seem acceptable. And if I wanted things to change, I would have to be the one to reset the balance.

It wasn't easy. I had to have conversations I dreaded. I told a colleague, "I need you to understand how much I'm juggling. I need help." I told a friend, "When you assume I'll always handle this, I feel unseen." Saying those words felt like peeling off protective skin. Vulnerable. But necessary.

Some people heard me. They apologised. They didn't realise the toll it had taken. We rebuilt stronger, with mutual respect. Others? They brushed it off. Told me I was being sensitive. And with them, I had to redefine the relationship. Not out of anger, but out of self-respect.

Spiritually, I was reminded that even Jesus stepped away from crowds that only wanted his miracles. Service without respect is not sustainable. Love without gratitude becomes exhausting.

Entitlement is corrosive. It eats away at joy, generosity, and trust. But gratitude is the currency that keeps relationships alive.

I began to spend more time with the unsung heroes in my life. The friend who always checks in. The colleague who sends handwritten thank-you notes. The family member who says, "I see how much you're doing." I started keeping a "gratitude jar" where I'd write down moments that refilled my emotional tank, a smile, a thank-you, a simple act of thoughtfulness.

One of the most moving moments came when my father, in a rare moment of clarity, looked me in the eye and said, "Thank you, my daughter. You've done more than I ever deserved." I wept. That sentence restored more than he could ever know.

There's a Shona proverb: "*Chawawadya chamuka.*" What you have eaten has already come alive. Taken in the positive it means: acknowledge what you've received from the investment made. Be grateful.

In leadership, I've seen the same truth. Teams thrive when people feel seen and appreciated. Marriages flourish when partners say thank you. Friendships deepen when we don't just assume, but honour each other's efforts.

So today I ask you: Are your relationships built on entitlement or gratitude? Are you teaching people to take from you without giving back, or are you modelling mutual respect?

You deserve relationships that replenish, not just ones that drain. Speak up. Celebrate those who show appreciation. And most of all, practise gratitude yourself. Let others know their kindness matters.

Relational wealth isn't just about giving endlessly. It's about creating a culture, at home, at work, in life, where people feel valued. Where love flows both ways. Where no one is taken for granted. That's the kind of wealth worth protecting.

CHAPTER 10

The Currency of Obedience, Redefining Success in the Kingdom

In a world that measures success in numbers, followers, impact, applause, it's easy to forget that the Kingdom of God counts differently. It's not the size of your platform that impresses heaven, but the posture of your heart. Not the reach of your voice, but the depth of your obedience.

There was a season in my life where everything looked fruitful on the outside. I was invited to speak, to lead, to mentor. My calendar was full, my inbox overflowing. And yet, I felt strangely disconnected. I realised I was performing purpose, not living it. I was more Martha than Mary, busy in the house of God but missing the presence of God.

The Bible tells us in 1 Samuel 15:22, "*Obedience is better than sacrifice.*" Yet so many of us sacrifice rest, intimacy, and joy on the altar of performance. We confuse being seen with being faithful. We assume that if it's public, it must be powerful. But some of the most powerful moves of God begin in hiddenness.

There were times I said yes to every opportunity, not because God told me to, but because I was afraid of being forgotten. I equated momentum with meaning. But God, in His mercy, pulled me back. He reminded me that in the Kingdom, fruit is not measured in applause, but in alignment. Success is not about how many listen to you,it's about how closely you're listening to Him.

Jesus often withdrew from crowds to pray. He walked away from attention to commune with the Father. Even at the peak of His ministry, He chose solitude over visibility. That alone redefines leadership.

We live in a culture addicted to visibility. We want our obedience to be seen, our impact to be celebrated. But the Kingdom honours the secret yes. The prayer whispered in private. The seed sown with no social media post, the quiet act of faithfulness.

I had to lay down the idol of being needed. I realised I was saying yes not just out of love, but out of fear,that if I didn't do it, no one else would. That if I stopped moving, I'd lose momentum. But true authority doesn't come from movement. It comes from abiding.

Abiding looks like turning down the stage to sit at Jesus' feet. It looks like declining the invitation when your soul is dry. It looks like trusting that God can use your silence as much as your speech.

I've come to see that spiritual authority is not loud. It's rooted. It's a woman who has been with Jesus and walks differently because of it. It's the one who obeys even when no one claps. The one who sows in tears and trusts God with the harvest.

Let us not trade intimacy for influence. Let us not confuse activity for fruit. Let us return to the place where obedience is the goal, and God's presence is the reward.

The Kingdom counts differently. And so must we. Reflection Questions:

- Am I confusing visibility with faithfulness?
- Have I made busyness my badge instead of obedience?
- Where is God calling me to be still, to say no, to trust Him in hiddenness?

This is the currency of the Kingdom: obedience. Let us spend it well.

CHAPTER 11

Resilience in the Valleys, Sustaining Your Heart through Hard Times

There is a quiet exhaustion that few talk about. It creeps in slowly, after the tenth phone call, the fifth family emergency, the endless deadlines, and the sleepless nights. And then one day, you walk into your house, close the door, and feel... empty. That's what happened to me.

Despite everything I teach about relational wealth, about love, boundaries, and giving generously, there came a moment when I had nothing left to give. My well was dry. My smile had become a mask. My prayers felt like echoes.

One day, I was rushing into the office when the security guard stopped me. "*Mhamha,*" he said kindly, "You're doing too much. Remember to rest." I laughed it off, but his words stayed with me. A stranger saw what I had refused to admit: I was exhausted.

That moment cracked something open in me. I went home that evening and sat in the quiet. For the first time in weeks, I didn't check my phone or make a list. I just breathed. And I wept.

In that valley, I began the slow work of healing. I stopped asking God for strength to keep going and started asking Him to heal what had already worn thin. I learned that resilience isn't about powering through. It's about pausing. Listening. Resting.

I began to care for myself the way I cared for others. I went for early morning work out sessions,those thrice-weekly bursts of motion became sacred. I took walks without my phone. I booked solitary retreats where no one needed me for anything. I returned to Scripture not as a task but as a refuge. I journaled, I cried, I prayed honest prayers, sometimes angry ones.

And I sought help. Counseling gave language to my weariness. Prayer groups became safe spaces. Friends who didn't demand anything from me sat beside me and held my silence. In those quiet, communal moments, I felt carried.

Leadership had taught me to be strong. Life taught me to be available. But this season taught me to be kind to myself. To see myself not as a machine but as a soul that needed tending. I remembered the story of Elijah, who ran until he collapsed under a broom tree. God didn't scold him. He gave him food, water, and rest. Even prophets need rest.

There's a Shona proverb: "*Chakatanga chasvika.*" What began has an end. The valley will not last forever. The wound may heal slowly, but it teaches. And when it heals, it leaves a scar, not of shame, but of wisdom.

I emerged from that valley not instantly whole, but deeply changed. I found joy in small things again. I began to say no without guilt. I began to lead from a place of overflow, not depletion. I remembered who I was beneath the roles and responsibilities.

To anyone in that valley today: you are not weak. You are human. You are worthy of rest, of care, of grace. Let others hold you when you cannot stand. Let God breathe new life into your spirit.

Resilience is not a badge for those who never break. It is the story of those who broke, rested, and returned. It is the quiet courage to hope again.

Isaiah 40:31 says, "*But those who hope in the Lord will renew their strength. They will soar on wings like eagles; they will run and not grow weary, they will walk and not be faint.*"

That is the promise. And that is my testimony.

Relational wealth is not built only in high moments. It is forged in valleys, in the fire of loss, the silence of burnout, and the long road back to joy. May you walk that road gently. May you come out stronger.

Part II: Banking on Relationships

CHAPTER 12

More Than Numbers

When I walked into my first bank as a young professional, I thought numbers were everything. Banking, after all, is built on figures, interest rates, balance sheets, profit margins, ratios. It is a world where precision is prized, where decimal points matter, where success seems to be measured in columns of black or red. As a young woman eager to prove myself, I poured my energy into mastering the numbers. I believed that if I could get the calculations right, if I could present flawless reports, if I could quote rates with confidence, then I would succeed.

And for a while, I did; numbers opened doors, and they earned me respect. They gave me credibility in meetings where I was the youngest, sometimes the only woman, and often underestimated. I remember the satisfaction of presenting figures that silenced doubters, of demonstrating mastery in a world where women were not always expected to excel. Numbers became my armour.

But it did not take long for me to realise that numbers alone were not enough. Because banking, beneath all its spreadsheets and statistics, is still about people. Behind every account number is a human being. Behind every loan is a dream. Behind every transaction is trust.

I learned this lesson in ways that surprised me. One of my earliest marketplace participants was a businessman with a modest portfolio. He was polite but cautious, always measuring his words. I approached him with efficiency, presenting figures and projections, thinking that data would win his trust. But he remained distant, reluctant to commit. One day, instead of rushing through numbers, I asked him about his business journey. He spoke for nearly an hour, about struggles, about risks he had taken, about his hopes for his children. Something shifted that day.

Our relationship changed. He began to trust me not because my numbers were different, but because I had listened. Years later, he told me that what convinced him was not my calculations but my care. That encounter was a turning point. I began to notice that the most successful bankers were not necessarily those with the sharpest technical skills, but those who built the strongest relationships.

Deals were won not on decimal points, but on trust. Loyalty was earned not through spreadsheets, but through presence. I began to understand that in banking, as in life, relationships are capital.

Relationships are incomplete until they are nourished. In banking, nourishment was not a plate of food, but it was time, attention, follow-up calls, remembering an individual's child's name, showing up at funerals, and celebrating milestones. These were the meals that fed trust. Without them, relationships starved, no matter how good the rates.

Numbers could attract marketplace participants, but relationships kept them. I saw colleagues who were technically brilliant but relationally careless. They treated marketplace participants as transactions, not people. They lost accounts as quickly as they won them. On the other hand, I saw bankers who remembered birthdays, who listened more than they spoke, who treated marketplace participants with dignity, and their portfolios grew steadily. Numbers matter, but relationships multiply.

Of course, this was not always easy. Banking is a high-pressure environment. Targets loomed. Bosses demanded results and time was short. It was tempting to reduce people to figures, to rush through interactions, to see marketplace participants as means to an end. But again and again, I was reminded that shortcuts eroded trust. And trust, once lost, was hard to regain.

Faith reinforced this conviction. Scripture spoke of loving your neighbour, of treating others as you would want to be treated. I began to see my work not just as a career, but as a calling. Every individual was a neighbour.

Every colleague was an opportunity to practice integrity. Every decision was a chance to demonstrate that relationships matter more than profit.

This perspective sometimes made me stand out. While others chased numbers at any cost, I found myself prioritising honesty, even when it meant losing short-term business. I remember one marketplace individual who wanted me to approve a loan I knew he could not sustain. The numbers said "yes," but the relationship, the bigger picture, said "no." Turning him down was hard. He was angry at first. But later, he returned and thanked me.

He said, "You saved me from myself." That experience taught me that caring for people sometimes means saying no. That too is relational wealth.

As indicated before, the Shona proverb: *"Rume rimwe harikombi churu."* One person alone cannot surround an anthill. I saw this truth in teams. Banking was not a solo endeavour. Success required collaboration with analysts, tellers, risk officers, and branch managers. I learned to value the invisible work of others, to build alliances, and to share credit. Teams thrived when relationships within them were strong. They fractured when competition replaced collaboration. Numbers alone could not sustain a team. Relationships could.

As I rose in the industry, the stakes grew higher. Portfolios expanded, marketplace participants became larger, and expectations increased. But the principle remained the same. The higher I went, the clearer it became: leadership is not about the numbers you produce, but about the trust you build. A team will follow a leader they trust through storms. An individual will stay with a banker they trust through downturns. Trust is the dividend of relational wealth.

Looking back, I see that my entire career was built on this discovery: numbers may open doors, but relationships keep them open. Numbers may impress in the moment, but relationships sustain over the years. Numbers may measure profit, but relationships measure legacy.

And so, when I say today that relationships are the world's real capital, I am not speaking abstractly. I am speaking from the dust of Mkoba and the polished floors of banks, from childhood lessons and the corporate marketplace, from the lives of marketplace participants who taught me that people remember presence more than profit.

Yes, numbers matter. They always will. But life, and leadership, is more than numbers. It is about people. It is about trust. It is about the capital of relationships, which outlasts every decimal point.

CHAPTER 13

The Master Key to Relationships

In banking, I often heard about the importance of keys. Keys to safes, keys to offices, keys to files. Each key carried responsibility, and losing one could have serious consequences. But over time, I discovered a different kind of key, one not made of metal, but of trust. I call it the master key: the relationship that opens many doors.

Looking back on my career, I can trace the turning points not only to my effort or talent, but to people who acted as master keys. Sponsors who mentioned my name in rooms I could not enter. Mentors who gave me wisdom that saved me from mistakes. Leaders who believed in me when others doubted. Each of these relationships unlocked opportunities that numbers alone could not.

My first master key came unexpectedly. I was a junior officer, working diligently but quietly, hoping that someone would notice. One day, a senior manager stopped me after a presentation. He said, "You have something. I want you to use it."

He began inviting me into meetings far above my rank, exposing me to marketplace participants and projects I never imagined handling so early. At the time, I thought it was simply luck. Now I know it was sponsorship. His belief in me became a master key that unlocked new rooms in my career.

There is a Shona proverb: "*Zano pangwa uine rako.*" Advice is valuable when you already have your own ideas. That manager's sponsorship was not a replacement for my effort; it was an amplifier. I had to bring my own preparation, my own integrity, my own work ethic. But his key fit doors I could not open alone. Together, my readiness and his sponsorship multiplied my opportunities.

Another master key was a woman I met later in my career. She had climbed the corporate ladder in a space where few women survived, let alone thrived. She saw in me a younger version of herself. She taught me how to navigate politics without losing integrity, how to build networks without becoming transactional, and how to balance family and career without burning out. Her guidance saved me from many pitfalls. She was not just a mentor; she was a compass. That relationship was a key that unlocked wisdom I could not have gained from textbooks.

Master keys are not always formal. Sometimes they come disguised as friendships. I remember a colleague who consistently shared information, encouraged me, and celebrated my wins even when he had nothing to gain. His generosity made my work lighter and my confidence stronger. He may not have opened doors to promotions, but he opened the door of encouragement, and that is no less valuable.

The danger, of course, is mistaking every relationship for a master key. Not everyone who smiles at you is trustworthy. Not every offer of help is genuine. I learned this painfully when I trusted people who later betrayed me, using my vulnerability against me. Those were not master keys but counterfeit ones, keys that seemed shiny but broke in the lock. From those experiences, I learned discernment. A true master key is consistent, selfless, and grounded in trust.

Faith helped me recognise the real keys. Scripture reminded me to pray for wisdom, to test spirits, to trust character more than charisma. Many times, I asked God to show me who was for me and who was not. Those prayers were answered in subtle ways: a word that revealed hidden motives, a nudge in my spirit, a truth exposed in time. Faith became the locksmith who helped me distinguish between keys that opened doors and those that led to traps.

As I advanced, I realised I too had to become a master key for others. Sponsorship is not only to be received; it must be given. I began to intentionally mention the names of younger professionals in rooms of opportunity. I mentored women who reminded me of myself at the start of my journey. I shared wisdom with those navigating the same storms I once faced. In doing so, I discovered a new truth: being a master key is just as fulfilling as finding one.

There is another proverb that says, "*Chara chimwe hachitswanyi inda.*" One finger cannot crush a louse. Alone, we are limited. Together, we are powerful. Master key relationships are proof of this. They remind us that no one rises alone. Every door we walk through was unlocked by someone who went ahead, who risked their credibility, who believed in us.

One of the dangers of success is forgetting the keys that opened our doors. Pride whispers that we arrived by ourselves, that our hard work alone explains our rise. But humility reminds us otherwise. I am who I am because of the master keys entrusted to me by others. To forget that would be to deny the truth of relational wealth.

What makes a master key so powerful is that it does not just open one door; it creates ripple effects. One sponsorship can lead to opportunities that multiply across a lifetime. One mentor's wisdom can shape decisions that influence generations. One friend's encouragement can give the strength to persevere through seasons of despair. Master keys are not small things. They are multipliers of destiny.

Today, when I speak of relational wealth, I always emphasise this principle: look for master keys, and be one. Nurture the relationships that open doors with integrity, and never take them for granted. And when you have climbed a little higher, turn and unlock doors for those behind you. Because the wealth of relationships is not in what we hoard, but in what we multiply.

Looking back, I can trace the arc of my journey through these keys:

- A senior manager who gave me opportunities.
- A woman leader who guided me through pitfalls.
- A colleague whose encouragement never wavered.
- A community of faith that prayed me forward.

Each one was a master key. Each one turned the locks that effort alone could not move. And each one taught me that relational wealth is not an abstract idea. It is real. It is practical. It is the difference between doors closed and doors opened, between isolation and opportunity, between surviving and thriving.

So I say with conviction: never underestimate the power of a master key relationship. Numbers will matter. Skills will matter. But the key that opens the door to your future will almost always be a person. Treasure them.

Honour them. And when it is your turn, become that key for someone else.

CHAPTER 14

When Relationships Become Capital

In banking, we were taught to view everything through the lens of capital. Money, land, machinery, even human effort, all of it could be measured, valued, invested, and multiplied. I absorbed this mindset early. It shaped how I approached portfolios, how I analysed risk, and how I presented opportunities. But somewhere along the way, I began to notice something the textbooks did not say: the most valuable form of capital was not always on the balance sheet. It was in the relationships.

At first, I saw it quietly, in the margins of my work. An individual who stayed loyal through years of ups and downs, not because of the best rates, but because of trust. A colleague who went out of their way to support me, not because they were paid extra, but because we respected each other. A mentor who invested time in me, not for personal gain, but because they believed in multiplying others. These moments didn't show up on quarterly reports, but they made all the difference.

And then it struck me: relationships are capital. They can be invested in, mismanaged, lost, redeemed, and multiplied. They carry risks and rewards. They can open doors or close them. They can bankrupt you emotionally, or they can make you wealthy in ways no bank account ever could.

I began to experiment with this idea. What if I thought of relationships as a portfolio? What if, instead of only tracking numbers, I tracked how I was investing in people? The metaphor grew richer the more I lived it. Some relationships are like savings accounts: steady, reliable, always there when you need them. Others are like high-risk investments: they promise much but can collapse suddenly. Some are like bad debts: draining, unhealthy, overdue for closure. Some are like hidden assets: undervalued, unnoticed, yet deeply significant.

When I began to frame relationships this way, I saw my life differently. I asked myself hard questions:

- Where am I making consistent deposits of time, kindness, and trust?

- Where am I overdrawn, expecting more than I have invested?

- Where am I carrying bad debts, relationships that drain but never replenish?

- Where am I ignoring hidden assets, people whose quiet support sustains me more than I acknowledge?

Those questions changed how I lived and led. They pushed me to invest in people with greater intentionality, to release relationships that were toxic, to celebrate the unsung heroes who were quietly sustaining me. They reminded me that wealth is not measured only in currency, but in community.

Faith deepened this framework for me. The Bible often uses financial language to describe relationships. We are told to forgive "debts," to store up "treasures in heaven," to invest our talents wisely. I began to see that God Himself views relationships as wealth. Love is the highest currency. Forgiveness is redemption. Kindness is a deposit that yields eternal dividends.

One story stands out in my memory. I was working with an individual whose business was struggling. Every number said we should withdraw, cut ties, and protect the bank's risk. But I knew the man behind the numbers. I had seen his integrity, his work ethic, and his resilience. I chose to advocate for him, not just on figures, but on the relationship. Years later, his business recovered, and he became one of our most loyal marketplace participants. That taught me that relationship capital is sometimes stronger than financial capital. Numbers rise and fall, but trust, once earned, compounds.

Another time, I faced betrayal in the marketplace, a colleague who undermined me to gain an advantage. It hurt deeply. At first, I thought of it only as a loss, a bad debt written into my account. But as I processed the pain, I realised it also taught me discernment. It sharpened my ability to read character, to test motives, to choose my investments more wisely. Even that scar became a seed, a loss that grew into wisdom.

Over time, I began to name my framework: the relationship portfolio. It is a way of thinking that has guided me ever since.

Just as bankers diversify assets, we must diversify relationships. Invest in family, friends, colleagues, mentors, faith communities. Do not put all your relational energy in one place. Just as investors review portfolios regularly, we must examine our relational lives. Where are we growing? Where are we depleting? Where do we need to rebalance?

As I grew into leadership, I began to teach this framework to others. I told young professionals: your greatest asset will not be your degree or your salary. It will be the trust you build, the network you nurture, the people who will speak your name in rooms you cannot enter. Those are your dividends. Those are your relational assets. Protect them. Invest in them. Honour them.

When I reflect now, I see that this way of thinking was not simply professional. It was personal. My mother's resilience, my aunt's open door, my neighbours' generosity, those were early deposits. My mentors, colleagues, and sponsors were assets that multiplied. My scars, betrayals, griefs, those were losses that became wisdom. My faith, that was the eternal account that steadied it all.

So yes, numbers matter. Strategies matter. But when I strip everything else away, I see clearly: relationships are the capital that sustains us. They are the wealth that outlasts every currency. They are the accounts we will look back on at the end of our lives, asking: Did I invest well? Did I make the right deposits? Did I multiply love?

Because in the end, when relationships are treated as capital, they reveal the true balance sheet of our lives. And that balance sheet does not lie.

CHAPTER 15

The Love Bank - Investing in Marriage and Family

You know what they teach you in banking? That the biggest account on day one isn't always the one that survives. I've seen million-dollar portfolios collapse within months. And I've seen modest accounts grow steadily for decades because someone kept making deposits, month after month, year after year.

Every day without a deposit is a day the balance shrinks. The deposits don't have to be dramatic. It's not about grand gestures or expensive gifts. It's simpler than that. Listening when you're tired. Choosing gentleness when you're provoked. Saying "I was wrong" quickly instead of letting it fester. Celebrating the small wins, a promotion, a good meal, and making it through a hard week together.

These feel small in the moment. But they compound. Just like interest in a savings account, these daily deposits add up to something that can sustain you through the inevitable storms.

My mother used to say this when neighbors shared meals, when families helped each other. At the time, I thought it was only about food. But it's deeper than that. You can't just assume a relationship will survive because you once made vows or signed a certificate. You have to keep feeding it.

Now, let me talk about extended family. Because this is where things get...complicated. I grew up believing that family bonds were automatic. Blood ties guaranteed loyalty, right? Your siblings, your parents, your cousins, they're family, so the relationship is just there, permanent, unbreakable. Life taught me otherwise.

I've seen cases where, when I need emotional, spiritual, or material support, I recall moments I would reach out to someone wanting solace or comfort. But alas, instead of receiving the listening ear I desperately needed, the response I received was a deluge of the listener's own predicaments, piling on their struggles, effectively setting aside or trivializing my issue. It's as if my pain became an invitation for them to unload theirs, leaving no space for mine to be held.

However, I've also seen some who have mastered something beautiful: the art of the strategic pulse-check call. They reach out with no specific agenda, no crisis to report, simply to say hello, to ask how you are and truly listen. These individuals understand the soft skills that drive sustainable relationship management. They know that relationships are not transactional ledgers but living ecosystems that need regular, genuine tending.

Here's what I had to learn, and I'm still learning it: love is not transactional, but relational wealth requires mutuality. I can't keep making withdrawals from my own well-being to fill everyone else's accounts. That's not sustainable. That's not wealth. That's heading toward bankruptcy.

Faith helped me see this differently. Jesus withdrew from crowds to rest. He said no to demands on His time when He needed to pray. He prioritized certain relationships without apology. That gave me permission,boundaries aren't betrayal. They're stewardship. They're protecting the accounts that matter most so they don't collapse.

I had to learn to say things I was afraid to say: "I can't help with that right now." "I need time to recharge before I can take on more." "I appreciate that you thought of me, but I have to prioritize my own family this season."

Those words felt like stones in my mouth the first time I said them. In our culture, saying no to family can be seen as selfish. As forgetting where you came from. But what I discovered,and this surprised me,is that when I protected my primary accounts, when I made sure my own marriage and children were not running on empty, I actually became a better daughter, a better sister, a better aunt. You can't pour from an empty cup. I know that sounds like something you'd read on Instagram, but it's true.

I recall attending a powerful marriage counseling session conducted by Mr and Mrs Kanokanga, where they introduced the concept of the 'love bank', the idea that in every marriage, there exists an emotional account between spouses. Every interaction, every word, every gesture is either a deposit or a withdrawal. Acts of kindness, patience, and attentiveness credit the account. Harsh words, neglect, or emotional injury debit it.

Over time, if withdrawals exceed deposits, the love bank becomes overdrawn, which is often what couples mean when they speak of 'irreconcilable differences'. The account is empty.

This framework resonated deeply with me, not only for marriage but for all relationships. We are always either building or eroding trust, always depositing or withdrawing.

Now, let's talk about forgiveness because this is where love banks get tricky. Every unresolved conflict is a debt left on the books. Small hurts compound into large resentments if you don't deal with them. The longer you wait to say "I was wrong," the higher the cost of reconciliation.

I learned this painfully. There were times I held onto hurts for weeks, even months, telling myself I was justified in my anger. And maybe I was justified. But that didn't change the fact that I was carrying a debt that was draining my love bank. Saying "I'm sorry" today is always cheaper than carrying that weight for months.

But, and this is important, forgiveness doesn't mean tolerating ongoing harm. I need to be clear about this because I've seen too many women, too many people, stay in relationships where the withdrawals never stop. Where apologies are empty words with no change in behavior. Where one person keeps trying to fill the account while the other keeps draining it without remorse.

That's not a marriage. That's martyrdom.

Love banks can be restored. I believe that. I've seen it. But only if both parties are willing to make deposits again. Only if there's genuine repentance, genuine effort, genuine change. If one person is pouring everything in while the other takes and takes and takes? At some point, you have to acknowledge that the account is closed. And that closing it might be the wisest thing you can do.

I know some of you reading this are in that place right now. Your love bank is overdrawn. You've been giving and giving until there's nothing left. And you're wondering: Is it me? Am I not doing enough? Should I try harder? Let me tell you something: Sometimes the most courageous thing you can do is stop trying to revive an account that the other person has abandoned. Sometimes protecting your own well-being, protecting your children, protecting your peace, that's not failure. That's wisdom.

So where does this leave us? I wish I could give you a formula. Five steps to a healthy love bank. Three keys to marital success. But I don't have that. What I have is this: Marriage certificates, birth certificates, family names, these things open accounts. But they don't sustain them.

Only consistent investment does. Only the daily choice to be kind. To forgive quickly. To show up, actually show up, not just be physically present. To celebrate each other. To protect the relationship when it's under attack, from stress, from busyness, from the world trying to pull you in different directions.

Over the years, I've witnessed the incredible impact of sharing, or not sharing, the day's highlights: those happy moments, those funny encounters, those sad experiences that color our daily lives. Continuous communication, the practice of bringing each other into the mundane and the meaningful, is a direct deposit into the love bank. It creates the closeness required in a marriage union.

Sharing vulnerabilities, being safe enough to expose situations that may be painful, admitting struggles, and confessing fears adds even more to that account. It says, 'I trust you with the tender parts of me.' And that trust, nurtured daily, becomes the foundation upon which everything else rests.

And then I have to choose. Do I let another day slip by, another withdrawal? Or do I pause, even for ten minutes, and invest? It's not sentimental. It's strategic. Because the love bank, with your spouse, with your children, with your family, is the most important account you'll ever manage. And here's the thing: you can't delegate it. You can't hire someone else to make those deposits for you. It's on you.

So where's your love bank today? Are you making deposits, or coasting on old investments? Are you taking more than you're giving? And in your extended family, are those relationships mutual, or have they become one-way streets?

I don't ask these questions to shame you. God knows I'm asking them of myself constantly. But I do think they're worth asking. Because at the end of our lives, when we look back, these are the accounts that will matter. Not our bank balance. Not our titles. Not our portfolios. The love we invested in the people closest to us. That's the wealth that endures.

CHAPTER 16

Unsavoury Moments and Invisible Debits

Every banker knows that a portfolio is not made up only of profits. There are losses too, bad debts, risky investments that fail, accounts that drain instead of grow. Relationships are no different. For all the master keys and loyal allies in my journey, there have also been unsavoury moments, invisible debits that took their toll.

They are not pleasant to recall, but they are part of the story. And without them, I would not have learned the wisdom that scars teach. One of my earliest lessons came from betrayal. I had worked tirelessly on a project, investing not only my skills but also my heart. I believed the colleague I worked with was an ally. We shared late nights, exchanged ideas, and encouraged one another. But when it came time to present, they claimed the credit. My name was barely mentioned. I sat in that meeting stunned, my heart pounding with disbelief.

The betrayal cut deeper than the professional loss. It was a personal debit, a withdrawal from the trust I had invested.

At first, I responded with silence. I swallowed the hurt, told myself to move on. But inside, I wrestled with anger and bitterness. Over time, I realised that carrying resentment was like carrying an overdraft: it weighed me down and drained my energy. Forgiveness did not mean excusing the betrayal, but it meant releasing myself from its grip. That experience seeded discernment in me. I learned to observe more carefully, to test loyalty, to build trust more slowly. The debit became an investment in wisdom.

There were other unsavoury moments too. Times when I faced open hostility in the marketplace. Times when male colleagues dismissed me before I spoke, or repeated my ideas as if they were their own. Times when office politics overshadowed integrity. Each moment was a debit, small on its own, but cumulative over time. They chipped away at my confidence, reminding me that not all environments are fair.

As shared before, the Shona proverb: "*Chakafukidza dzimba matenga.*" The roof covers the secrets of homes. In the marketplace, the roof also covers the secrets of the marketplace. What is visible on the outside often hides the tensions within. I learned that behind polished presentations and polite smiles, there could be envy, rivalry, even sabotage. Those were invisible debits, drains on trust that did not show up on reports, but were felt deeply in the atmosphere.

And sometimes, the unsavoury moments came from my own missteps. I recall a time when, under pressure, I snapped at a junior colleague. It was uncharacteristic of me, but the stress of deadlines had made me harsh. The look on their face haunted me. I realised then that I had made a withdrawal from their trust, a debit I had to repair.

I apologised, sincerely, and worked to rebuild that relationship. It taught me that leaders are not exempt from causing harm. We, too, can leave scars. That awareness made me more cautious, more intentional in my words.

Some debits were more subtle. Relationships that drained without ever replenishing. People who took my time, my energy, and my ideas, but rarely gave back. At first, I tolerated them, thinking generosity meant endless giving. But over time, I learned the importance of boundaries. Every portfolio needs limits. Without them, even the wealthiest account will be depleted. Setting boundaries was not selfish; it was stewardship. It allowed me to invest in relationships that bore fruit instead of those that only consumed.

Faith reframed even the ugliest debits. Scripture spoke of loving enemies, of blessing those who curse you, of forgiving seventy times seven. These were not easy commands, but they freed me. They reminded me that my wealth is not in what others give me, but in what I choose to give. That perspective turned some of my deepest debits into opportunities to deposit grace.

Yet I will not romanticise these moments. They hurt. Betrayal, hostility, exploitation, they leave marks. They remind us of the risk inherent in every relationship. And sometimes, despite our best efforts, we lose. Some relationships end in bankruptcy. Some scars remain tender; that is reality.

But here is what I have come to believe: even unsavoury moments can be redeemed. Even invisible debits can teach us something. They can sharpen our discernment. They can deepen our empathy. They can humble us, reminding us that we are all capable of harm.

They can push us closer to God, reminding us that His account of love never runs dry.

When I look at my relational portfolio today, I see both the credits and the debits. I see betrayals that became lessons, politics that became resilience, missteps that became humility, and toxic ties that became boundaries. I see a balance sheet that is not perfect but honest. And in that honesty, there is wealth.

Because in the end, relational wealth is not about never losing. It is about learning from every withdrawal. It is about choosing not to let unsavoury moments define us. It is about trusting that even the invisible debits can become invisible dividends in time.

The Human Balance Sheet

Every banker learns to read a balance sheet. It is the snapshot of a business at a given moment, assets on one side, liabilities on the other, equity at the bottom. It tells the truth about financial health. You can argue with projections, but the balance sheet does not lie.

For years, I read balance sheets with diligence. I analysed numbers, probed discrepancies, and looked for hidden risks. It was my job to see not only what was presented but what was concealed. Yet somewhere along the line, I began to wonder: if we could draft balance sheets for people, for leaders, for ourselves, what would they look like?

Because the truth is, each of us carries a human balance sheet. We have assets, trust we have earned, love we have given, skills we have cultivated. We have liabilities, grudges we carry, relationships we have neglected, harm we have caused. And we have equity, the net worth of who we are when everything else is stripped away.

This idea came alive for me one day in a meeting. The numbers on the page suggested caution. The company's assets looked strong, but the liabilities were growing. Yet when I looked at the leadership team, I saw something else. Their cohesion, their shared trust, their vision for the future, these were assets no balance sheet could measure. And I realised: the real bottom line is not only in numbers. It is in people.

There is a Shona proverb: "*Chinokanganwa idemo asi muti haukanganwi.*" The axe forgets, but the tree remembers. Our human balance sheets carry memory. We may forget moments where we hurt others, but they remember. Our liabilities do not disappear simply because we choose to ignore them. They stay on the sheet until we make amends.

I began to reflect on my own human balance sheet. What assets had I built? Loyalty from marketplace participants. Trust from colleagues. Friendships that had endured. Wisdom gained through scars. These were intangible, but they were real. What liabilities did I carry? The times I had spoken harshly. Relationships I had neglected. People I had failed to notice. These were uncomfortable to admit, but they were necessary for honesty. And what was my equity? It was not my title or income. It was my character. The net worth of who I was when no one was watching.

The metaphor grew richer as I lived it. Just as businesses need regular audits, so do we. We must pause and examine our lives. Are we growing our relational assets? Are we ignoring liabilities that need addressing? Are we increasing our equity in integrity, humility, and love?

Faith deepened this reflection for me. Scripture speaks of treasures in heaven, of giving an account of our lives, and of love being the greatest commandment. God Himself keeps a kind of balance sheet. And His measure is not the size of our portfolios but the depth of our relationships. Love credited, forgiveness extended, kindness given, these are the assets He values. Pride, bitterness, selfishness- these are liabilities that weigh us down.

I remember a colleague who was technically brilliant but relationally bankrupt. He delivered numbers but left a trail of broken trust. His assets were impressive on paper, but his liabilities eroded them. In the end, his equity was thin. He taught me that skill without integrity is like a balance sheet heavy with debt. It cannot sustain.

On the other hand, I remember a cleaner in one of our branches. She was not on the payroll of executives, but she was rich in relational assets. She greeted everyone with kindness, remembered names, and comforted those who were stressed. People gravitated toward her warmth. Her financial income was small, but her relational wealth was vast. Her human balance sheet was strong. She reminded me that equity is not measured in status but in substance.

There is another proverb: "*Ushe madzoro hunoravanwa.*" Leadership is like a relay; it is passed on. Our human balance sheets are not only personal; they are generational. The assets we build or the debts we leave will affect those who come after us. That is why relational wealth is so critical. It outlasts us. It becomes legacy.

In my own journey, I have tried to live with awareness of this balance sheet. To celebrate the assets, loyal friendships, moments of forgiveness, and trust that endured. To confront the liabilities, apologies owed, pride surrendered, lessons learned. And to protect my equity, the integrity that remains when titles fade, and applause stops.

When I mentor younger professionals, I encourage them to start their own audits. I ask: Who are your relational assets? Who has invested in you, and how are you honouring them? Where are your liabilities? Who have you hurt, and how are you making it right? What is your equity? What do you want to be remembered for when the numbers no longer matter?

The beauty of the human balance sheet is that it is dynamic. Liabilities can be reduced through forgiveness. Assets can grow through intentional investment. Equity can increase through daily choices. No one is stuck with their first draft. We can all revise our sheets, one relationship at a time.

So, when I say that relationships are the world's real capital, this is what I mean. They are the assets that sustain us, the liabilities that challenge us, the equity that defines us. They are the true bottom line.

And at the end of our lives, when no one is asking about our net worth or balance sheets in the bank, this will be the question: What does your human balance sheet say? Did you invest in love? Did you settle your debts with forgiveness? Did you build equity in integrity and compassion? Because of that, in the end, is the only balance sheet that matters.

CHAPTER 18

Politics in the Marketplace

Every organisation has a marketplace. It may not always be a polished table with leather chairs, but it is there, the place where decisions are made, where power is negotiated, where voices are amplified or silenced. When I first entered those spaces, I thought merit would speak for itself. I thought numbers and performance would win the day. I quickly learned otherwise.

Politics is the undercurrent of every marketplace. It is the unseen force shaping what is said and what is decided, the hidden hand behind alliances and rivalries. At first, I resisted the very idea. "I will not play politics," I told myself. But soon I realised that refusing to acknowledge politics is not the same as escaping it. Whether you play or not, you are still on the board. The question is not whether politics exists. The question is how you navigate it.

One of my earliest lessons came in a meeting where a proposal I had worked on was up for discussion. I had prepared thoroughly, every figure in place, every risk addressed. Yet as I spoke, I could feel the resistance.

Not because the idea was flawed, but because of who had spoken before me and where the alliances in the room lay. A more senior colleague, whose support I had not secured beforehand, subtly undermined my work. The proposal stalled. That day, I understood: in the marketplace, content matters, but context matters more.

There is a Shona proverb: "*Hanzi kune anekutya hapana anopedza.*" To the one feared, no one dares to finish their food. Power shapes behaviour. In the marketplace, power often spoke louder than ideas. I saw how some people's words carried weight, even when they were vague. I saw others dismissed, even when they were brilliant. Politics determined whose plates were left untouched and whose were cleared.

At first, this disillusioned me. It felt unfair, even corrupt. But with time, I realised that politics is not always malicious. At its root, it is about relationships, who trusts whom, who feels threatened, and who feels supported. It is about egos and insecurities, but also about alliances and shared visions. Once I saw it this way, I could engage without losing my integrity.

I learned the importance of preparation beyond numbers. Before presenting in the marketplace, I began to engage stakeholders one-on-one. I listened to their concerns, built trust, and sought allies. By the time I entered the room, I was not alone. I had voices ready to support me. That was not manipulation; it was a relational strategy. It was ensuring that my ideas had the backing they deserved.

I also learned the value of silence. Sometimes the wisest move in a political space is not to fight every battle, but to wait, to observe, to choose your moment. I remember one meeting where heated arguments swirled around the table. I stayed quiet, listening. Near the end, I spoke calmly, weaving together the points that had been made, offering a way forward. The room settled. The decision moved in the direction I had hoped. Later, someone told me, "You won the room because you did not fight it." That taught me that influence is not always loud. Sometimes it is quiet and steady.

There were moments when politics turned ugly, when egos clashed, when people undermined one another, when alliances became toxic. Those moments were draining. They reminded me that not every relationship is an asset. Some are liabilities. Some cost more than they give. Navigating those situations required discernment: knowing when to engage, when to step back, when to draw boundaries.

My faith anchored me in those spaces. Scripture reminded me that promotion comes not from east or west, but from God. That truth freed me from desperation. I did not need to compromise my values to gain favour. I could trust that integrity would speak louder in the long run. Politics could delay me, but it could not deny me if God had opened the door.

There is another proverb: "*Hombarume huru inokandira zvayo kure.*" A skilled hunter throws his spear far. Politics is about trajectory. Some battles are about today, but the wise see the long game. I learned to ask: Is this argument worth my energy? Will it matter in five years? Sometimes the answer was yes, and I fought. Sometimes it was no, and I let it go. That discernment saved me from many unnecessary wounds.

Over time, I realised that politics in the marketplace is not only about survival. It is also an opportunity. If you understand the dynamics, you can build bridges. You can become the person who diffuses tension, who connects rivals, who earns trust across divides. That is relational capital at its highest form: turning politics into partnership.

One story stays with me. A colleague who had opposed me fiercely in meetings approached me privately one day. "You are different," they said. "You do not humiliate me when you disagree. You listen. That's why I can work with you." That moment shifted our dynamic. What had been rivalry became collaboration. It taught me that politics does not have to be destructive. It can be redirected.

Today, when I mentor others stepping into leadership, I tell them: do not be naïve about politics. Do not assume that merit will always win. But also, do not sell your soul to the game. Learn the dynamics. Build allies. Choose your battles. Lead with integrity. And above all, remember that relationships are the real capital. Politics is simply the arena where that capital is tested.

Because at the end of the day, politics will always be part of the marketplace. But those who rise above the noise, who navigate with wisdom, who invest in trust, will find that even in the mess of egos and alliances, there is opportunity. And the leaders who endure are those who understand that power is temporary, but relationships endure.

CHAPTER 19

Authenticity
in the Marketplace

In the early days of my career, I thought success meant becoming what others wanted me to be. The industry was dominated by men, most of them older than me, most of them sure of their place. I was young, female, and new. To survive, I thought I had to adjust, to blend in, to mute the parts of myself that stood out. So I dressed like them, spoke like them, even adopted their rhythms of conversation. I thought authenticity was a luxury I could not afford.

For a while, it worked. I gained respect, earned promotions, and ticked the boxes of success. But inside, something was withering. I would come home exhausted, not just from work, but from pretending. I was living two lives: the one that was accepted in the marketplace and the one that was truly me. And the gap between them grew heavier by the day.

There is a Shona proverb: "*Chokwadi hachiputirwi mudumbu.*" The truth cannot be swallowed forever. My true self could not remain hidden indefinitely. One day, in a meeting, I slipped. Instead of my carefully polished corporate tone, I spoke with warmth, using a proverb my mother had taught me. To my surprise, the individual leaned forward, interested. They said, "I like how you put that. It makes sense." That moment cracked something open. Authenticity, I realised, was not a liability. It was an asset.

From then on, I began to experiment. Instead of suppressing my background, I drew from it. I used stories from Mkoba to illustrate resilience. I quoted proverbs to explain strategy. I spoke openly about my faith when appropriate, not to preach, but to be honest about what grounded me. And again and again, I saw the same reaction: people leaned in. Authenticity connected where polish alone could not.

It was not always easy; there were colleagues who thought I was naïve, who whispered that I was "too open." There were moments when my authenticity cost me opportunities because I refused to play games. But I had tasted the freedom of alignment, of being the same person in the marketplace and at home, and I could not go back.

Authenticity also made me a better leader; people trust what is real. They can sense pretense, even when it is polished. When I admitted mistakes, my team grew closer. When I acknowledged pressure instead of pretending it didn't exist, they felt seen. When I shared parts of my story, they shared theirs. Authenticity built bridges faster than authority ever could.

My faith gave me courage in this journey. Scripture reminded me that I am fearfully and wonderfully made, that God does not make mistakes, that my story is not an accident. If God had entrusted me with my background, my scars, my culture, then hiding them was not humility, it was a waste. Authenticity was stewardship. It was bringing my full self to the table as an offering.

One story remains vivid. I was in a high-stakes negotiation where the other side was pressing hard. The room was tense, full of jargon and posturing. Instead of matching their energy, I paused and told a short story about my childhood in Mkoba, about how resilience and partnership had always been more powerful than rivalry. The atmosphere shifted. The conversation softened. We found common ground. Later, a colleague told me, "That story won them over. They saw you as real." That moment reminded me that authenticity disarms. It invites connection.

Of course, authenticity is not recklessness. It is not about saying everything that crosses your mind. It is not about exposing yourself without wisdom. It is about alignment. About ensuring that the self you bring to work is not a costume but a true reflection of your values. It is about consistency, the same person in the office, at home, and in prayer.

As I reflect now, I see that authenticity in the marketplace is not just about personal well-being. It is relational capital. People are drawn to what is real. Marketplace participants trust authenticity more than rehearsed lines. Teams follow authentic leaders more than polished ones. Colleagues collaborate more easily with those who are genuine. Authenticity multiplies trust, and trust multiplies influence.

When I mentor younger professionals, especially women, I tell them: do not trade your authenticity for acceptance. Yes, you will feel pressure to conform. Yes, the system will test you. But the very things you are tempted to hide, your culture, your faith, your story, may be the things that set you apart. They may be your master key.

Looking back, I am grateful for the unsustainable weight of pretense, because it forced me to choose authenticity. And I am grateful for the courage God gave me to walk in it, even when it cost me. Because in the end, authenticity gave me more than promotions ever could. It gave me peace. It gave me freedom. It gave me the ability to look in the mirror and say: I am the same person in every room. That, to me, is true wealth.

CHAPTER 20

Pressure Cookers and Gentle Souls

Corporate life can feel like a pressure cooker. The deadlines, the targets, the constant competition, all of it builds heat. Add egos, politics, and personalities to the mix, and the environment can feel like it is about to explode. I lived much of my career in that kind of atmosphere. Meetings where voices were raised, the marketplace where tempers flared, offices where the stress was so thick you could feel it in the air.

At first, I thought the way to survive was to toughen up, to match the heat with my own fire. If someone shouted, I would shout louder. If someone pressed me, I would press back. For a while, it worked. I won a few battles and proved that I could hold my ground. But I soon realised that fighting heat with heat only made the room hotter. It drained me, hardened me, and did little to create lasting solutions.

It was then that I began to discover the power of gentleness. Not weakness, not passivity, but the kind of gentleness that steadies storms. The kind that lowers the temperature in the room. The kind that allows pressure cookers to release their steam without exploding.

I remember one meeting in particular. A senior executive was furious about missed targets. He berated the team, his voice rising, his words cutting. Everyone sat frozen, afraid to respond. My instinct was to shrink, to stay invisible. But instead, I took a deep breath and spoke calmly. "We hear your frustration. Let's look at what can be salvaged and what can be done differently going forward." The words were simple, but the tone shifted the room. The shouting subsided. The conversation moved to solutions. Later, a colleague whispered, "You calmed him down. You saved us." That was the day I learned that gentleness can be more powerful than force.

There is a Shona proverb: "*Nyorondokunatsa, kuipandokukanganisa.*" Gentleness builds; harshness destroys. I saw that truth lived out again and again. Harshness might produce quick compliance, but it rarely produces commitment. Gentleness, on the other hand, built trust. It created space for collaboration, for creativity, for loyalty. It made people want to show up, not just because they had to, but because they felt respected.

Of course, gentleness does not mean being a pushover. In fact, it often requires more strength than anger. It means holding your ground without raising your voice. It means staying calm when others lose control. It means choosing patience when provoked. It is strength under control, not strength out of control.

Faith helped me see gentleness as strength. Scripture spoke of a "gentle answer turning away wrath" and of the fruit of the Spirit being gentleness. Jesus Himself, strong enough to command storms, chose gentleness in the face of betrayal. If He could lead with gentleness, then surely I could too.

But gentleness was not only for others; it was also for myself. I had to learn to be gentle with my own heart, not to drive myself into the ground with impossible expectations. The pressure cooker was not only external; it was internal. The voices that told me I had to prove myself, to be perfect, to always perform, those were pressures I placed on myself. Learning gentleness meant learning rest. It meant remembering that my worth was not tied to my productivity, but to who I was.

Some of the greatest leaders I admired carried this quality. They were not the loudest in the room, but when they spoke, people listened. They carried a presence that calmed storms, that reassured teams, that made people feel safe even in crisis. They showed me that leadership is not about controlling others, but about controlling yourself.

One story illustrates this well. We were negotiating a high-stakes deal with multiple parties. The room was tense, with each side digging in. I watched as one leader listened patiently, nodded thoughtfully, and then spoke with quiet authority. His words were measured, his tone steady. The atmosphere shifted. Agreement became possible. That day, I saw that gentleness is not passive. It is persuasive.

Over time, I came to see that pressure cookers are inevitable in leadership. There will always be deadlines, conflicts, disappointments. The question is not how to avoid them, but how to respond. And the answer, I discovered, is emotional intelligence, the ability to understand, manage, and channel emotions, both yours and others'. Gentleness is one of its greatest expressions.

When I mentor younger professionals, I tell them: do not confuse harshness with strength. Do not confuse loudness with influence. True strength is calm under pressure. True influence is steady in storms. Gentleness may not make headlines, but it builds legacies.

Looking back, I see that the pressure cookers of my career were not wasted. They tested me, refined me, and taught me that relational wealth is built not in easy moments, but in heated ones. Anyone can be kind when things are smooth. It takes courage to be gentle when the heat is on.

And perhaps that is the lesson I carry most deeply: pressure will always come. But if you choose gentleness, with others and with yourself, you can transform pressure into purpose. You can turn volatility into trust. You can leave behind not scars of harshness, but seeds of healing. Because in the end, the leaders who endure are not those who shout the loudest, but those who carry gentle souls into pressure cookers and change the atmosphere.

CHAPTER 21

Unsung Heroes

When people look at a career from the outside, they see the highlights, the promotions, the awards and the polished photos in newspapers or on LinkedIn. They see the results and assume those results came from one person's brilliance or hard work. But I know better. My journey was never a solo effort. Behind every success, there were countless others holding me up. People without titles, without recognition, without applause, but without whom I could not have stood. They are my unsung heroes.

I think first of the assistants. In every branch, in every office, there were men and women who kept the engine running. They organised schedules, prepared documents, and fielded calls. Their work was often invisible, taken for granted, but it was the glue that held everything together. I remember one assistant in particular who stayed late many nights, not because it was required, but because she didn't want me to face deadlines alone. She reminded me that loyalty is not written in contracts, but in quiet sacrifices. She was never mentioned in annual reports, but she was part of my success story.

Then there were the cleaners, people who swept floors, emptied bins, and made sure the office was welcoming every morning. It is easy to overlook them, to rush past with barely a greeting, but I tried never to forget. I remembered their names, asked about their families, and noticed their faithfulness. And I discovered something remarkable: the cleaners often knew more about the true atmosphere of the marketplace than anyone else. They saw who smiled, who frowned, who stayed late, and who left early. Their quiet presence was an anchor. One cleaner once said to me, "We pray for you." Imagine that someone unseen by the world covering me in prayer. That is wealth no spreadsheet can measure.

I mention again, there is a Shona proverb: "*Munhu munhu nekuda kwevanhu.*" A person is a person because of other people. It echoes the African philosophy of Ubuntu: *I am because we are.* My unsung heroes embodied this truth. They reminded me that identity and achievement are not individual, but communal. My "I" was always sustained by a "we."

Mentors were another category of heroes. Some were official, assigned to guide me. Others emerged naturally, noticing my potential and choosing to invest in me.

They gave me advice when I was confused, correction when I was wrong, encouragement when I was weary. They risked their own credibility to recommend me for opportunities. They whispered truths I needed to hear: "You belong here," "Don't give up," "Remember who you are." Their voices steadied me when self-doubt shouted louder.

Then there were the prayer warriors, people who may never have understood the details of my work, but who lifted me before God. My mother, of course, was chief among them. Her whispered prayers were the foundation of my journey. But there were also friends, church members, even strangers who said, "We are praying for you." Their intercession created a covering, a hedge of protection I cannot quantify but cannot deny. Many times, I faced storms that should have drowned me. Yet I stayed afloat. I believe it was because unseen hands were holding me in prayer.

Colleagues who acted as encouragers were heroes too. Not everyone was competitive. Some chose generosity over rivalry. They shared knowledge, celebrated my wins, and spoke truth when I doubted myself. One colleague made it his mission to encourage younger staff. His words were simple: "You're doing well," "That was a good presentation", but they landed like water on dry ground. Encouragement is free, yet it is one of the most valuable currencies of relational wealth.

Faith taught me to see these people not as background figures but as gifts. Scripture speaks of the body having many parts, each important. The eye cannot say to the hand, "I don't need you." The head cannot dismiss the foot. In the same way, leaders cannot dismiss those who seem "small." Every role is vital. Every person carries dignity. And often, the ones least noticed carry the heaviest weight.

One story remains vivid. During a particularly stressful quarter, I was juggling demanding marketplace participants and intense board meetings. My stress showed. One day, a security guard at the bank stopped me as I rushed in. He looked me in the eye and said, "You're doing too much. Remember to rest." He didn't have a degree in leadership. He didn't know the details of my calendar. But his words pierced through the noise. That moment reminded me that wisdom is not confined to titles.

Sometimes, it is spoken by those who guard doors and sweep floors.

Unsung heroes also reminded me of humility. Success is intoxicating. Applause can make you believe the illusion that you did it all. But when I looked around, I saw too many hands holding me up to believe that lie. Gratitude became my antidote to pride. I made it a practice to thank people: the assistant, the cleaner, the guard, the colleague. I wrote notes, offered words, remembered birthdays. Not as a strategy, but as sincerity. Because gratitude is also relational wealth. It deepens bonds, strengthens loyalty, and honours dignity.

When I mentor others now, I urge them: do not overlook the unsung heroes in your journey. Notice them. Honour them. Invest in them. Because leadership is not about standing alone at the top; it is about acknowledging those who lifted you there. And one day, when history is written, it will not only be the leaders who matter. It will be the quiet ones who kept the lights on, the faithful ones who prayed, the generous ones who encouraged.

Looking back, I see my success not as mine alone, but as ours. It belongs to the assistants who stayed late, the cleaners who prayed, the mentors who guided, the prayer warriors who interceded, and the colleagues who encouraged. They were not on magazine covers. Their names may never appear in history books. But they are inscribed in my story, in my heart, in the balance sheet of relational wealth that I carry.

And perhaps that is the truest measure of wealth: not what we achieve alone, but what we achieve together with those who may never be applauded, but who make all the difference.

Part III: The Human Advantage

CHAPTER 22

The Human Advantage in a Digital Age

When I first entered the marketplace, technology was already reshaping the way we lived and worked. Emails replaced letters, spreadsheets replaced ledgers, and later, smartphones replaced so many of our conversations. Today, we stand in an age where artificial intelligence can draft reports, machines can analyse data faster than humans ever could, and automation has made entire job categories obsolete. In many industries, efficiency and speed are prized above all else.

And yet, the more I watched this transformation unfold, the more convinced I became of something incredible: the more digital the world becomes, the more valuable the human touch becomes.

Algorithms can process information, but they cannot offer empathy. Machines can execute transactions, but they cannot build trust. Artificial intelligence can predict patterns, but it cannot nurture belonging. The one thing technology cannot replicate is the heart, the uniquely human ability to connect, to comfort, to collaborate.

I saw this truth vividly during the COVID-19 pandemic. Overnight, meetings went virtual. Colleagues became faces on screens. marketplace participants became voices on calls. The human cues we relied on, body language, energy in the room, and shared silences, disappeared. At first, we celebrated the efficiency: no travel, no commutes, no wasted minutes. But soon the cracks appeared. Misunderstandings multiplied. Isolation deepened. Mental health declined. People were more "connected" than ever digitally, yet lonelier than ever relationally.

In that season, I realised that leaders who thrived were not the ones who mastered technology, but the ones who mastered humanity. The managers who checked in not only about targets but about families. The colleagues who sent a message just to say, "How are you coping?" The leaders who admitted their own struggles, creating space for others to breathe. Those were the ones whose teams stayed loyal, whose organisations endured. It was not efficiency that saved them; it was empathy.

Technology does not change that truth. If anything, it highlights it. We remain human only because of the relationships we cultivate. No digital platform can replace that.

I recall an individual conversation during the pandemic that cemented this truth for me. The individual said, "We know you cannot change the market for us, but we appreciate that you call just to check how we are coping." That call had no immediate financial return. But it built trust that no algorithm could measure. Months later, when the market began to recover, the individual brought more business to the bank. Relational wealth had sustained where financial projections had faltered.

Faith also framed this lesson for me. Scripture speaks of us being created in the image of God, relational beings, designed for connection. That design does not fade with technology. If anything, it becomes more vital. Machines can mimic many things, but they cannot mimic love. They cannot replicate grace. They cannot embody the divine spark that makes us human.

Of course, I am not against technology. It has brought incredible efficiency, innovation, and access. But it must serve humanity, not replace it. Too often, I have seen leaders hide behind screens instead of showing up in person. Too often, I have seen people chase efficiency at the cost of empathy. When that happens, we become poorer, not richer.

There is another proverb: "*Kandiro kanoenda kunobva kamwe.*" One dish is returned, where another comes from. Relationships are reciprocal. Machines cannot reciprocate love. They cannot return kindness. Only humans can. That is why, in a digital age, the leaders who will endure are those who remember that relationships are capital, not code.

When I mentor younger professionals navigating this new landscape, I encourage them: yes, master the tools, but do not lose the touch. Learn the systems, but also learn the souls of people. Technology may open doors, but trust keeps them open. Machines may provide data, but only humans can provide dignity.

Looking back, I see clearly: the human advantage is not in competing with machines, but in cultivating what machines cannot. Empathy. Presence. Belonging. Love. These are not "soft" skills. They are strategic assets. They are the capital that will outlast every wave of disruption.

So when I say that relationships are the world's real capital, I mean it even more in this digital age. Because at the end of the day, when the systems crash, when the algorithms fail, when the machines malfunction, it is people who will carry us through. It is the hands that hold us, the voices that comfort us, the hearts that believe in us. That is the wealth that endures. That is the human advantage.

CHAPTER 23

Gadget Etiquette in Relationships

There was a time when relationships were marked by presence, by looking into each other's eyes, by lingering in conversation, by truly listening. Today, presence is often divided. We sit across from one another with phones on the table, notifications buzzing, attention split between the human being in front of us and the screen in our hand. The gadgets that promised to connect us have, in many ways, disconnected us.

I first noticed this shift in the marketplace. Meetings where participants glanced down every few minutes, checking messages as if the conversation in the room were secondary. Others were responding to emails while someone else was speaking. I remember someone presenting at a conference and realising that half of them were scrolling through their phones. I continued listening, but inside I wondered: how much are we losing when we cannot give one another full attention?

The same pattern appeared outside of work. Families gathered at dinner tables with everyone on their devices. Friends meeting for coffee, each taking turns to check social media instead of engaging. Even in church, I watched as people followed sermons on their phones, only to be distracted by other notifications. The irony is sharp: the very tools designed to enhance communication were eroding our ability to be fully present.

There is a Shona proverb: "*Kugara hunzwanana.*" To dwell together is to understand one another. True understanding requires presence. You cannot truly know someone if you are only half with them. Gadgets have made us physically together but mentally absent. That absence chips away at trust, at intimacy, at the sense of being valued.

In banking, I learned how much marketplace participants noticed the presence. Some bankers prided themselves on multitasking, typing emails while marketplace participants spoke, glancing at screens during meetings. I chose a different path. I put my phone away, looked people in the eye, and listened. Time and again, marketplace participants later told me, "You were different. You actually listened." It wasn't my rates they remembered. It was my attention. Presence was my competitive edge.

At home, I had to face the same lesson. There were evenings when I returned from long days at the marketplace, only to continue scrolling through my phone while my family tried to talk to me. One night, my child said, "Mama, you're not really here." The words pierced me. I realised I was cheating them of the very thing I preached to others: relational wealth. From that day, I became intentional about putting my phone aside during meals, about choosing presence over distraction.

It was not always easy, but it was necessary.

Faith speaks to this, too. Jesus was often surrounded by crowds, pulled in every direction. Yet when He stopped for an individual, He gave them full attention. He looked at people. He listened to them. He noticed them. That presence transformed lives. If the Son of God thought presence mattered, who am I to treat it lightly?

There is another proverb: "*Meso anokuudza.*" Eyes will tell you. Presence allows us to read what words cannot say, the fatigue in someone's posture, the sadness behind a smile, the excitement in their eyes. Gadgets steal that wisdom. A text cannot replace the weight of eye contact. An emoji cannot capture the nuance of emotion. We need presence to truly see one another.

Of course, gadgets are not evil. They connect families across continents, provide information at our fingertips, and allow us to work efficiently. I am grateful for them. But they must serve relationships, not sabotage them. They must be tools, not masters.

So how do we reclaim presence in a gadget-saturated world? For me, it began with small disciplines. Phones away during meals. No devices in certain rooms. Scheduled "unplugged" times, where I gave myself permission to disconnect in order to connect. In meetings, I learned to model this by closing my laptop when others spoke. At home, I practised listening with my eyes, not just my ears. Over time, these small habits made a big difference.

When I mentor younger leaders, I encourage them: make your presence your edge. In a world where everyone is distracted, full attention is rare and powerful. Be the person who looks up, who listens fully, who makes others feel seen. That is relational capital that gadgets cannot compete with.

I also tell families: give each other the gift of undivided attention. Phones can wait. Notifications can wait. But moments cannot. Children grow, loved ones age, conversations pass. Once missed, they cannot be reclaimed. Presence is the currency of love.

Looking back, I see that gadgets are not the enemy. The enemy is inattentiveness. The temptation to give others only half of ourselves. The lie that multitasking builds efficiency, when in fact it erodes trust.

The future will only bring more technology, more devices, more distractions. But the leaders, families, and friendships that endure will be those that practice gadget etiquette, the discipline of presence. Because at the end of the day, the greatest gift we can give one another is not a message sent or a post liked. It is our full selves. It is presence. And that presence, more than any gadget, is what nourishes relationships into real wealth.

CHAPTER 24

Grief, Loss, and the
Gift of Empathy

Grief is the shadow no one wants to face, yet it visits us all. It does not knock politely; it enters uninvited, rearranging everything. I have walked through grief, and it has marked me. But it has also given me a gift I did not expect: empathy.

My first real encounter with grief was losing family members I loved dearly. Death was not an abstract concept; it was an empty chair at the table, a silence in conversations, a voice I longed to hear but could not. At first, I tried to be strong, to push the pain aside, to keep going as if nothing had changed. But grief does not let itself be ignored. It waits, heavy, until you face it.

There is a Shona proverb: "*Rufu haruna ndarira.*" Death has no trumpet. It does not announce itself. It arrives suddenly, cutting across our plans, reminding us that life is fragile. Each time it came, I felt a wound deeper than words could express. And yet, even in the sorrow, I found lessons that shaped me.

The first lesson was presence. In grief, words often fail. What mattered most were not speeches but people who showed up. A neighbour who sat quietly beside me. A friend who brought food without asking. A colleague who simply said, "I'm here." Those simple gestures taught me that presence is more powerful than perfection. I carried that lesson forward: in times of loss, do not strive to fix, just be there.

The second lesson was empathy. Until you have faced loss yourself, it is easy to underestimate the pain of others. You may say the right words but miss the weight of the wound. My own grief changed that. It softened me. It made me slower to judge, quicker to comfort. It made me attentive to silences, to the small signs of sorrow that others carried. It gave me the ability to walk gently with those who grieved, because I knew the terrain myself.

Faith gave me hope in grief. I held onto Scriptures that spoke of eternal life, of God wiping away every tear, of mourning turned into dancing. These promises did not erase the pain, but they gave it context. They reminded me that grief was not the end of the story. I clung to the image of Jesus weeping at Lazarus' tomb, proof that even God incarnate did not rush past grief, but entered it fully. That gave me permission to feel my own sorrow without shame.

In the marketplace, grief shaped me as a leader. I began to see that colleagues are not just employees; they are people carrying invisible burdens. Some had lost parents, others children, others marriages. Their performance was not only about skill, but about the weight they carried. Grief gave me compassion in how I led, patience in how I judged, and humanity in how I responded. It made me the kind of leader who asked, "How are you, really?" and meant it.

I recall one colleague who returned to work just days after losing a loved one. They tried to act as if nothing had happened, but their eyes told the truth. I sat with them privately and said, "You don't have to be strong for me. Take the time you need." They broke down in tears. Later, they told me those words gave them permission to grieve. That moment reminded me: empathy does not remove the pain, but it shares it, and that sharing lightens the load.

There is another proverb: "*Moyo muti unomera paunodyarwa*." The heart grows where it is planted. Grief planted my heart in the soil of empathy. It forced me to grow in ways I never planned. It expanded my capacity to feel, to notice, to care. And that growth became one of my richest forms of relational wealth.

Of course, grief is not linear. Some days I felt strong; other days, undone by a memory, a song, a place. I learned to accept that grief is not something you "get over." It becomes part of you. But that part can make you more human, not less. It can deepen your appreciation for life, sharpen your sense of priorities, and remind you of what truly matters.

When I mentor others, I often tell them: do not rush past grief. Do not numb it or bury it. Let it teach you. Let it soften you. Let it turn you outward toward others. Because grief, if embraced, becomes empathy. And empathy is one of the greatest gifts a leader, or a friend, or a parent, can carry.

Looking back, I see that grief has been both my heaviest burden and my greatest teacher. It stripped away illusions of control, reminded me of life's brevity, and carved empathy into my heart. It made me treasure relationships more deeply, because I know how quickly they can be gone.

It made me invest more intentionally in people, because tomorrow is never guaranteed.

Faith tells me that one day, grief will end. That there will be no more tears, no more loss, no more separation. Until then, I carry the scars of grief as seeds of compassion. They make me more attentive, more tender, more human.

And so, when I speak about relational wealth, I do so not only from moments of joy, but from valleys of sorrow. Because in those valleys, I discovered the truth: wealth is not what we accumulate, but the love we give and receive. And grief, painful as it is, reminds us of that truth more clearly than anything else.

CHAPTER 25

Ubuntu for the World

The older I grow, the more I realise that the lessons of my childhood in Mkoba were not small or provincial. They were seeds of wisdom that the whole world needs. What we in Africa call *Ubuntu* is more than a cultural practice. It is a philosophy of life, a way of being human, a truth that every society can learn from: "*I am because we are.*"

In Mkoba, Ubuntu was not a theory. It was a lived reality. When one family lacked food, another shared. When someone fell ill, neighbours cared for the children. When a funeral came, the whole community gathered, not just to mourn but to support. We did not survive as individuals; we survived as a network. That interdependence was so normal to me that I only realised its uniqueness later, when I entered worlds where independence was prized above all.

Identity is not self-made; it is relational. Wealth is not accumulation; it is contribution. Success is not rising alone; it is rising together.

As I stepped into the corporate world, I found a stark contrast. The systems I encountered often prized competition over collaboration, individual achievement over collective good, and efficiency over empathy. People were taught to look out for themselves, to climb ladders even if it meant stepping on others. On the surface, it seemed effective. But beneath, it bred isolation, distrust, and fragility.

That was when I began to see the gift of Ubuntu. What if leaders understood that relationships are the foundation of resilience? What if companies measured success not only by profit, but by community impact? What if nations valued dignity as much as Gross Domestic Product (GDP)? Ubuntu offers a blueprint for a fractured world, not as a nostalgic idea, but as a practical strategy for thriving.

During the COVID-19 pandemic, this truth became even clearer. The virus reminded us that independence is an illusion. No matter how wealthy or powerful a nation, it could not survive alone. We were connected by invisible threads. My health depended on your choices, your safety on mine. Ubuntu was not just an African philosophy; it was a global reality.

I remember watching communities across Africa mobilise during the pandemic. People shared food, pooled resources, and looked after the vulnerable. They did not wait for governments or systems; they leaned into Ubuntu. The world could have learned so much from that.

Faith resonates with this truth, too. Scripture describes us as the body of Christ, many parts, one body. No part can say to another, "I do not need you." The hand needs the eye, the eye needs the foot, the foot needs the ear.

This is Ubuntu in spiritual language. We are incomplete without one another.

One story illustrates this power. A colleague from another culture once asked me how I built such loyalty in my teams. I told him, "Because I treat them as family, not just staff." He was surprised. He had been taught to keep strict boundaries, to separate personal from professional. But he later admitted, "Your way works. People trust you. They give more because they feel you are with them, not above them." That was Ubuntu in practice, leadership as shared humanity.

Remember the proverb: "*Chara chimwe hachitswanyi inda.*" One finger cannot crush a louse. It takes many fingers working together. Ubuntu reminds us that problems too big for individuals can be solved when communities unite. Whether it is poverty, climate change, or injustice, the solution is never a lone genius. It is always collective wisdom.

The danger today is that we are building societies that reward isolation. We glorify the self-made individual, forgetting that no one is truly self-made. We celebrate independence, forgetting that our survival depends on interdependence. Ubuntu challenges that narrative. It calls us back to what is real: our humanity is bound together.

When I speak to global audiences, I often tell them: the world is rediscovering what Africa never forgot. In an era of loneliness, Africa offers belonging. In an era of competition, Africa offers collaboration. In an era of efficiency, Africa offers empathy. This is our gift to the world, not as charity, but as wisdom born of survival.

I do not romanticise Ubuntu. I know our communities also carry flaws, exclusion, patriarchy, and politics. Ubuntu is not perfect. But at its heart, it carries truths that transcend cultures: we need one another, we thrive in connection, we are diminished when we diminish others.

When I mentor leaders, I encourage them to practice Ubuntu not only as philosophy but as a daily discipline. Notice the people others overlook. Share credit generously. Build systems that include rather than exclude. Make decisions not only for today, but for generations. These are not soft gestures. They are strategic moves. In a fractured world, Ubuntu is not a weakness. It is a competitive advantage.

Looking back, I see that Ubuntu shaped me long before I named it. It was in the meals shared in Mkoba, the neighbours who carried one another's burdens, the elders who spoke proverbs into our lives. Those early experiences gave me a lens I carry into every marketplace, every conversation, every vision for the future.

And looking forward, I believe Ubuntu is Africa's greatest export. We may not always lead in technology or wealth, but we carry relational wisdom the world desperately needs. The future will not be secured by stronger machines or bigger profits. It will be secured by stronger communities. That is Ubuntu. That is relational wealth on a global scale.

So when I say, "I am because we are," I am not only recalling my childhood. I am offering the world a truth I believe with all my heart: humanity cannot survive as fragments. We must rediscover the wealth of relationships, the power of connection, the gift of belonging. Ubuntu is not just for Africa; it is for the world.

CHAPTER 26

From Scar to Strategy

For many years, I wanted to hide my scars; they felt like marks of weakness, reminders of pain I wished I could forget. The world celebrates strength, not wounds; perfection, not imperfection. In the marketplace and leadership circles, vulnerability often feels dangerous. Yet as my journey unfolded, I discovered a paradox: my scars were not liabilities, they were strategies. Every scar carried a story, and every story carried wisdom.

The scar of my childhood, growing up in a home marked by both love and strictness, taught me empathy. It gave me a sensitivity to suffering that no textbook could provide. As a child, I thought that pain diminished me. But later, I saw that it sharpened my ability to notice when others were hurting. It gave me the instinct to ask questions others overlooked, to offer kindness others forgot. In leadership, that sensitivity became strategy. It made me a leader who could see the invisible burdens people carried, and that awareness built loyalty, trust, and commitment.

The scar of exclusion, being left out of games, overlooked in school, and underestimated in the marketplace, taught me the power of belonging. Those wounds could have left me bitter. Instead, they made me determined to create spaces where others felt included. They became the foundation of my leadership philosophy: that people thrive when they feel they belong. This was not just a personal value; it was a strategic advantage. Teams that felt safe and seen performed better. Marketplace participants who felt valued stayed loyal. Inclusion was not sentiment; it was strategy.

The scar of betrayal, colleagues who claimed credit for my work, alliances that turned into rivalry, taught me discernment. Betrayal hurts because it strikes at trust. But it also teaches you to watch more carefully, to test more deeply, to rely less on appearances and more on character. Those scars became a filter, helping me distinguish between allies and opportunists. That discernment saved me from costly mistakes and allowed me to invest in relationships that truly mattered.

The scar of grief, losing people I loved, softened me. It reminded me that life is fragile, that tomorrow is not guaranteed. It changed the way I led. I no longer saw colleagues only as employees; I saw them as human beings carrying silent sorrows. Grief deepened my patience, my compassion, my presence. And that presence built relational wealth in ways profit never could.

As mentioned before, the Shona proverb: "*Chitsva chiri murutsoka.*" What is new is found in your own footsteps. My scars were footsteps I never would have chosen, but they led me to new wisdom I could not have found otherwise. Each scar became a seed. Each seed became a strategy.

At first, I thought strategy came only from skills, training, and planning. But life taught me that strategy also comes from scars. Because scars are proof that you have survived. They are maps of resilience. They are reminders that pain can be transformed into purpose.

Faith reframed this truth for me most powerfully. I thought often of Jesus after the resurrection. His scars were not erased. He still bore them in His hands and side. But those scars were no longer wounds; they were testimonies. They were the marks that convinced Thomas to believe. In the same way, I realised my scars were not something to be hidden, but testimony to be shared. They could build faith in others, show resilience, and invite trust.

One story stays with me. I was mentoring a young woman who felt discouraged, convinced she was failing. Instead of giving her a list of instructions, I shared some of my own scars, times I was overlooked, moments I almost gave up. Her eyes widened. She said, "I thought you had it all together. Hearing your struggles makes me believe I can make it too." That day, I saw clearly: scars connect us more than successes ever could.

There is another proverb: "*Mhandu yakanaka haiperi.*" A good enemy never disappears. Challenges will always come. But scars teach us how to face them with wisdom. They become part of our armour. Not armour that hardens us, but armour that remembers: I survived before, I will survive again.

As I reflect on my journey, I see a pattern. Pain became purpose. Scars became strategies. What felt like loss became lessons.

And those lessons gave me credibility in leadership, not because I was flawless, but because I was real.

This is why I say that relationships are capital. They are not made only in the easy times. They are forged in scars, in reconciliations after betrayal, in bonds deepened by grief, in trust restored after mistakes. Scars make relationships stronger, not weaker, when we allow them to heal with honesty.

When I speak to leaders today, I urge them: do not hide your scars. Use them. Let them guide your strategy. Share them wisely, not recklessly, but enough to remind people you are human. Enough to remind your teams that perfection is not required, but resilience is. Enough to show that survival is strength, and healing is possible.

Because in the end, leadership is not about pretending you have never been hurt. It is about showing how you turned hurt into wisdom, wounds into strategies, scars into seeds. That is the wealth scars can give us.

And when I look at my own balance sheet, I see scars not as liabilities, but as assets. They are proof that I have lived, that I have endured, that I have learned. They are the capital that cannot be stolen, the strategy that cannot be copied. From scar to strategy, that has been my journey. And it is the journey I offer to others: that even the most painful marks can become your greatest source of wisdom, strength, and relational wealth.

CHAPTER 27

Passing the Baton

Every race has a moment that defines it: the handover. In a relay, no matter how fast the runner is, no matter how much ground they cover, the team will lose if the baton is dropped. Passing the baton is not simply about running; it is about trust, timing, and transfer. The same is true in life and leadership.

I often think of my own journey as a relay. I did not begin the race alone. Others ran before me, preparing the way. My mother, with her prayers and resilience, carried the baton of faith and endurance. My mentors carried the baton of wisdom and guidance. My colleagues carried the baton of collaboration and support. They placed it in my hands, and I have run my leg of the race as faithfully as I could. But I know that my part is not the finish line. My calling is not only to run well, but to pass the baton to others.

There is a Shona proverb: "*Ushe madzoro hunoravanwa.*" Leadership is a relay; it is shared in turns. This wisdom is often forgotten in the marketplace, where leaders cling to power, afraid to let go.

But true wealth, relational wealth, is not measured by how much you hoard. It is measured by how much you release, by the legacy you leave in others.

I remember mentoring a young professional early in her career. She was talented, but hesitant, doubting whether she belonged in the competitive world of finance. I saw in her a spark that reminded me of myself years earlier. I took time to guide her, to open doors for her, to mention her name in rooms she could not yet enter. Years later, she rose to a position of influence and sent me a message: "Thank you for believing in me before I believed in myself." That, to me, was passing the baton.

But passing the baton is not always easy. It requires humility, it requires letting go of ego, acknowledging that we are not irreplaceable. It requires trust, believing that others will carry forward what we began. And it requires timing, knowing when to release, when to empower others, when to let another shine

I have seen the pain when batons are not passed well. In both the marketplace and public life, I have watched leaders who refused to prepare successors, who held onto positions long past their season, believing that only they could carry the vision forward. But history teaches us otherwise. No matter how gifted the leader, no matter how significant their contributions, there comes a time when the baton must be passed.

I have seen this pattern across nations, across industries, across generations, leaders who confused their identity with their position, who feared that stepping aside meant becoming irrelevant. But the opposite is true. The leaders who are most remembered are not those who cling longest to power, but those who raised up others to go further than they themselves could go.

As mentioned earlier the proverb : *"Kandiro kanoenda kunobva kamwe."* One dish goes where another comes from. Giving creates cycles of receiving. Passing the baton ensures continuity. When we invest in others, we ourselves are enriched. Our legacy becomes larger than our lifespan.

The tragedy is not in stepping down. The tragedy is in holding on so long that what could have been a graceful transition becomes a painful extraction. The tragedy is in disciples who never become leaders because their mentor would not release them. The tragedy is in wisdom that dies with its keeper because they never found it worthy to share.

In my own career, I have been deliberate about sponsorship. Not just advising people, but actively advocating for them, creating opportunities, transferring social capital. Because I know that the true measure of leadership is not what I achieve alone, but what continues after me. Titles fade. Portfolios close. But people endure.

CHAPTER 28

The Trust Dividend

In banking, we spoke often about dividends. Dividends are the returns you receive from investments, evidence that your capital has not only been preserved but multiplied. marketplace participants celebrated when dividends were declared, because they proved that their patience and discipline had paid off. Dividends are a sign of growth, of value, of reward.

Over time, I began to see that relationships also pay dividends. But the greatest one of all is trust. Trust is the compound interest of relational wealth. It multiplies over time, quietly but powerfully. And when it is present, it sustains relationships through storms that would otherwise destroy them.

Trust is not built overnight. It is like a long-term investment. You deposit honesty, consistency, and presence again and again. At first, the returns seem small, almost invisible. But over time, trust compounds.

It grows silently in the background until one day you realise that it has become your greatest asset.

I learned this lesson in the most practical ways with marketplace participants. Some stayed with me for years, even when competitors offered slightly better rates or faster turnaround times. When I asked why, they often said, "Because we trust you." That trust was the dividend of years of showing up, keeping promises, and listening carefully. It was not something I could produce instantly with a clever strategy. It was the return on steady, faithful deposits over time.

But just as trust compounds, betrayal destroys. One broken promise can wipe out years of deposits. I saw this painfully in the marketplace. A colleague who lied to secure a deal lost not only the deal but the confidence of marketplace participants for years to come. It was like a financial scandal, a single act that bankrupted a reputation. Rebuilding took far longer than the act of destruction. That experience taught me never to gamble with trust. It is too precious, too fragile, too foundational.

Faith reinforced this. Scripture says, "*He who is faithful in little will be faithful in much.*" Trust grows in the small things, in being on time, in keeping confidences, in following through. People watch the little things more than we realise. And those small deposits of faithfulness add up to massive dividends over time.

One story stays vivid in my memory. I had someone whose company faced a financial storm. They called me, not because I could change the market, but because they trusted I would walk with them. We spent hours strategising, encouraging, sometimes simply sitting in silence together. Years later, when their fortunes turned, they brought me opportunities I could never have asked for.

Trust had carried us through the valley and paid dividends on the mountaintop.

Trust is communal; it does not live in isolation. It grows when people carry one another, when communities share burdens, when teams protect each other's reputations. Trust multiplies in circles, not silos.

But trust also demands courage. It requires us to risk vulnerability. To trust others is to hand them part of your heart, knowing they could drop it. Many fear this risk and choose control instead. But I have learned that without risk, there is no trust, and without trust, there is no depth. Shallow relationships may be safe, but they yield no dividends. Only trust produces lasting returns.

In leadership, the trust dividend is what sustains influence. Teams do not follow titles; they follow trust. Marketplace participants do not stay for contracts; they stay for trust. Organisations do not endure because of products alone; they endure because stakeholders believe in their integrity. Trust is not just moral; it is strategic. It is the dividend that determines long-term sustainability.

I also discovered that trust has a spiritual dimension. Trust in God became the foundation of my resilience. When circumstances were uncertain, when doors closed, when betrayal stung, I had to decide: would I trust? Would I believe that God was still working, even when I could not see? That trust, too, paid dividends. It gave me peace in storms, hope in grief, and courage in uncertainty. It became my deepest wealth.

Looking back, I see that every stage of my journey was marked by trust dividends:

- Childhood, trusting neighbours to share, and seeing how the community carried us.
- Career, trusting mentors and sponsors, and reaping opportunities.
- Leadership, trusting teams with responsibility, and seeing them flourish.
- Faith, trusting God with my scars, and receiving peace that surpasses understanding.

Trust does not make life easy. It makes life deep. It multiplies what matters most: loyalty, love, resilience. It produces dividends that no market crash can erase, no betrayal can permanently bankrupt, and no system can replace.

When I mentor others now, I tell them: make trust your greatest investment. Guard it fiercely. Deposit it daily. Never gamble with it. Because when all else fades, the trust dividend will remain.

And at the end of our lives, when balance sheets and portfolios no longer matter, the question will be simple: Did people trust you? Did you build equity in love, integrity, and faith? Did you leave behind dividends of trust that others can spend long after you are gone? That is the real wealth. That is the return worth living for.

CHAPTER 29

Capital of Connection

In every industry I worked in, people spoke about capital. Financial capital. Political capital. Human capital. We analysed it, pursued it, and guarded it. But over time, I came to see that there is another kind of capital that is far more enduring, far more powerful, and far more necessary: the capital of connection.

Connection is what makes us human. It is the invisible thread that ties us to one another, the current that flows beneath every relationship, the currency that cannot be printed but must be cultivated. When the connection is strong, people thrive. When it is broken, people wither.

I saw this truth early in life. In Mkoba, connection was our wealth. Neighbours who shared food, families who carried one another's burdens, children who played together without asking about titles or income, these were our riches. We had little in material terms, but we had much in connection. And that connection sustained us.

Later, in the corporate world, I saw how easily connection was sacrificed. Meetings became battles for dominance. Colleagues competed for recognition. Leaders retreated behind titles. Efficiency became more important than empathy. And slowly, the capital of connection eroded. People became lonely in crowded offices, unheard in endless meetings, unseen in polished reports. I learned that disconnection is not the absence of people; it is the absence of being known.

There is a Shona proverb: *"Kugara hunzwanana."* To dwell together is to understand one another. Connection requires more than proximity. It requires presence, listening, and curiosity. It is not enough to sit at the same table; we must hear each other's hearts. Without that, proximity becomes emptiness. With it, proximity becomes power.

I recall one individual who struggled to trust banks because of past disappointments. For months, he kept me at arm's length. Numbers alone could not win him. But slowly, through genuine interest, through remembering his stories, through consistent follow-up, a connection formed. One day, he said, "Now I know you are not only my banker, but you are my partner." That moment of connection turned a hesitant individual into a loyal ally. The capital of connection outlasted the competition.

Connection also shaped the way I led. I discovered that teams do not give their best to leaders who are distant. They may comply, but they will not commit. True commitment comes when leaders connect, when they notice birthdays, ask about families, acknowledge struggles, and celebrate wins. Those small gestures may seem insignificant, but they are deposits in the bank of connection. And those deposits yield exponential returns.

Faith resonates with this truth deeply. God Himself chose connection. He did not remain distant; He came near. Emmanuel, God with us. Scripture speaks of us being one body, one family, one people. The Gospel is, at its heart, a story of connection restored: between God and humanity, and between humanity and one another. If connection is God's strategy, then surely it must be ours too.

Remember the proverb: "*Chara chimwe hachitswanyi inda.*" One finger cannot crush a louse. Alone, we are limited. Together, we are strong. Connection multiplies strength, resilience, and creativity. It allows us to accomplish what no individual can.

But I must also be honest: connection requires risk. It requires vulnerability. It means letting others see not only your strengths, but also your weaknesses. It means risking disappointment, betrayal, even heartbreak. Many avoid connection because of that risk. But I have learned that the greater risk is disconnection. A life without connection may be safer, but it is emptier. A leader without connection may avoid betrayal, but they also forfeit loyalty.

Over the years, I came to see that connection is not a soft concept. It is strategic capital. Nations rise or fall on the strength of connection. Organisations endure or collapse depending on whether people feel connected to a shared purpose. Families thrive or fracture depending on whether connection is nurtured or neglected. Connection is not optional; it is essential.

One story illustrates this vividly. During a particularly difficult season, I was under immense pressure. Deadlines loomed, politics swirled, my own energy was depleted. One evening, as I prepared to leave the office, a colleague knocked and said, "I just wanted to check if you are okay." That question, so simple, carried immense weight. It reminded me that I was not alone. It renewed my strength. That moment of connection cost nothing but yielded everything.

When I mentor others now, I encourage them to think of connection as capital. Ask yourself: how much have I invested in being truly present? How much have I withdrawn through distraction or neglect? Where am I overdrawn? Where am I rich? These questions are not sentimental; they are strategic. Because the capital of connection is what sustains leaders, organisations, and communities when everything else fails.

Looking back, I see that my wealth is not measured in money or titles. It is measured in connection, in the people who call me friend, in the marketplace participants who still trust me, in the colleagues who still reach out years later, in the family who knows me deeply. That is my account of true capital.

And looking forward, I believe this is what the world needs most. In an age of loneliness, connection is wealth. In an age of division, connection is healing. In an age of speed, connection is an anchor. Because in the end, when all other currencies lose value, the connection remains. It is the capital that sustains, the wealth that multiplies, the treasure that endures.

CHAPTER 30

Legacy Accounts

In banking, legacy accounts are not the ones you spend from daily. They are the ones you establish for the future, accounts that outlast immediate needs, that hold wealth for generations. They are not flashy, but they are enduring. In many ways, my whole philosophy of relational wealth comes down to this: what are we depositing into the accounts that will outlast us?

I think often about my mother. She did not leave behind a fortune in money. What she left was far more enduring: a legacy of faith, resilience, and kindness. Those were her deposits into my life, and they continue to yield dividends decades later. She built a legacy account that I now draw from every day.

There is a Shona proverb: *"Zviuya hazvienzani nezvawakasiya."* What you leave behind is greater than what you enjoyed in the moment. Legacy is not about consumption; it is about contribution. It asks us to shift our gaze from what we achieve for ourselves to what we leave for others.

In my own journey, I came to see that titles fade. Positions end. Even wealth can vanish. But the deposits of love, trust, and wisdom we place into others endure. When I left roles I once thought were central to my identity, I discovered that what remained were not the achievements but the relationships. The people who called, the colleagues who still reached out, the young professionals who said, "You shaped me." That was my real account.

Legacy accounts are built daily. Every act of kindness, every word of encouragement, every moment of integrity is a deposit. Every betrayal, every harsh word, every neglect is a withdrawal. Over time, the balance tells the truth. You cannot fake a legacy. It reveals itself in what remains after you are gone.

Faith sharpens this truth. Scripture speaks of treasures in heaven, accounts where moth and rust cannot destroy, where thieves cannot break in. Those treasures are not money; they are relationships. Love given, forgiveness extended, service offered, these are eternal deposits. When I think of legacy this way, I realise that my true wealth is not stored in banks but in heaven, not measured in currency but in lives touched.

One story illustrates this for me. Years after I had moved on from a particular role, I received a message from a young woman I had mentored. She wrote, "I still remember your words when I almost gave up. You may not know it, but they kept me going." That message reminded me: legacy is not always visible now. It shows up years later, sometimes when you least expect it.

In the corporate world, I also saw leaders who understood legacy and those who did not. Some clung to power, hoarded knowledge, and left behind empty departments when they moved on. Others invested in people, shared wisdom freely, and left behind thriving teams. The difference was stark. The first group's achievements ended with them. The second group's legacy lived on. That contrast shaped me deeply. I knew which kind of leader I wanted to be.

Legacy is also communal. It is not only about individual impact, but about systems and cultures we leave behind. I often ask myself: have I built structures that empower others, or ones that depend only on me? Have I multiplied leadership, or have I hoarded it? The answers to those questions reveal whether my deposits are for myself or for the future.

Grief, too, reframed legacy for me. When loved ones died, I thought first of what I had lost. But over time, I began to see what they had left. The laughter, the lessons, the resilience, the faith. Death could not erase those deposits. They lived on in me, in my family, in all who knew them. That comforted me. It reminded me that our lives echo beyond our years.

When I mentor others now, I tell them: measure your success not only by what you accomplish, but by who rises after you. Ask yourself: who am I mentoring? Who am I advocating for? Who am I equipping to carry the vision forward? Who will continue this work when I am gone? Because the race is not about individual speed, it is about collective finish.

The tragedy is not in leaders who serve long seasons, but in leaders who fail to build the capacity in others to carry the torch forward. When we invest in developing those around us, we ensure that the vision outlives us. When we focus only on our own tenure without preparing successors, we risk watching years of progress unravel the moment we can no longer lead. The question is not when to leave, but whether we are continuously raising up those who can continue and even exceed what we began.

Looking back, I see my life not only as a journey of roles and achievements, but as a portfolio of legacy accounts. Some were built intentionally, others unconsciously. But together, they form the wealth I will leave behind. And I pray that wealth will be measured not in titles or trophies, but in people, in stronger leaders, in wiser communities, in deeper faith.

Because in the end, the truest question is not what we earned, but what we left. Not how much we consumed, but how much we contributed. Not the size of our paychecks, but the size of our deposits in the lives of others.

That is legacy. That is wealth. That is the account worth building.

CHAPTER 31

The Future Is Relational

When I look at the world around me, I see great change. Technology is advancing at a pace we can barely keep up with. Economies rise and fall overnight. Nations are more connected than ever, yet more divided than ever. In such a world, many ask: what will secure the future? Will it be innovation? Wealth? Power?

I believe the answer is simpler, and yet more incredible: the future is relational.

We are entering an era where relationships will determine resilience more than resources, where trust will determine influence more than titles, and where connection will determine wealth more than currency. It may sound idealistic, but I have seen the evidence in my own life and work: relationships outlast everything else.

As the world fractures under the weight of inequality, climate change, pandemics, and politics, survival will depend on interdependence. No nation, no organisation, no individual can thrive alone.

In banking, I saw this principle play out repeatedly. Marketplace participants with vast financial portfolios sometimes collapsed because they lacked relational resilience. They burned bridges, eroded trust, and when storms came, they stood alone. Others with smaller portfolios endured because they had strong networks, trusted allies, and loyal relationships. It became clear: in the long run, relational capital sustains more than financial capital.

The COVID-19 pandemic was a global case study in this. Nations with the best healthcare systems still struggled if their citizens did not trust their leaders. Organisations with cutting-edge technology still faltered if employees felt unseen. Families with resources still broke apart if the connection was absent. The virus was indiscriminate, but resilience was relational.

Faith amplifies this truth. Scripture tells us that love never fails. Prophecies, tongues, and knowledge will all pass away. But love endures. That is God's way of saying: the future is relational. It is not what we build, but how we build together. It is not what we know, but how we love. It is not what we possess, but what we share.

"Chara chimwe hachitswanyi inda." (a proverb we mentioned in another chapter) means that one finger cannot crush a louse. The future is too complex for lone heroes. We need teams, communities, and networks. We need relational ecosystems, not just individual stars. The leaders who will thrive tomorrow are those who can build bridges, weave alliances, and sustain trust across divides.

The younger generation understands this instinctively. I watch how they build communities online, how they value collaboration over hierarchy, how they care about belonging as much as achievement. They are telling us something: the future is not only about being the best. It is about being connected. It is about building circles, not thrones. But I must also issue a caution: the future being relational does not mean it will automatically be so. It requires intentionality. It requires us to invest in empathy, to practice presence, to build trust. It requires leaders to unlearn isolation and embrace interdependence. It requires systems that reward collaboration, not just competition.

When I mentor leaders today, I ask them: what are you building for the future? Are you investing only in products and systems, or also in people and relationships? Are you preparing successors, or clinging to power? Are you measuring success only in profit, or also in trust? These are not sentimental questions. They are strategic ones. Because the future will belong to those who understand that relationships are capital.

Looking back, my life has convinced me of this: relationships sustained me when money could not, when systems failed, when grief overwhelmed me. They were my real wealth. And looking forward, I am convinced of this: relationships will sustain the world in the same way.

The future is relational, not because it sounds good, but because it is true. It is written in our proverbs, proven in our crises, affirmed in our faith, and lived in our daily lives. The question is not whether relationships will matter in the future. The question is whether we will choose to invest in them now.

So as I think about legacy, about what I want to leave behind, this is the conviction I carry: teach people to treasure relationships as capital. Teach leaders to build trust as a strategy. Teach communities to practice Ubuntu as survival. Teach families to prioritise presence over distraction. Teach nations to value dignity over dominance. Because this is the path forward.

And when the future comes, with its technologies, its challenges, its opportunities, those who have invested in relational wealth will be ready. They will not just survive. They will flourish, because the future is not financial. The future is not technological. The future is not political. The future is relational.

CHAPTER 32

A Heart for Relationships

As I look back over the path of my life, the laughter and the tears, the triumphs and the scars, the marketplace and the backrooms, the villages and the cities, one theme stands above them all: relationships. They have been my greatest teachers, my deepest pain, my richest reward, and my most enduring wealth.

I was born into a family where love and struggle lived side by side. I grew up in a community where neighbours shared what little they had, teaching me that survival is communal. I stepped into a career where numbers were prized, only to discover that people mattered more. I walked through betrayals, through grief, through victories, and through valleys, and in all of it, one truth never let me go: relationships are the world's real capital.

When I began writing, I thought I was simply collecting articles and notes from a career in finance and leadership. But as I reflected, I realised I was tracing something deeper: the heart that carried me through it all. A heart for relationships.

This heart has not always been easy to carry. It has been wounded by betrayal, misunderstood in the marketplace, underestimated in competitive spaces. There were times when I wished I could harden it, become indifferent, protect myself by caring less. But I could never stay in that place. My heart always returned to what it knew to be true: that life is richer when we love, that leadership is stronger when it is relational, that faith is deeper when it is shared.

Faith has been the anchor of this heart. The God I serve is relational at His core, Father, Son, and Spirit in eternal communion. His greatest commandment is to love Him and to love one another. His Son, Jesus, came not only to save but to connect, to reconcile, to restore broken relationships. That divine heart for relationships has shaped my human one.

I have seen enough of the world to know that titles fade, wealth shifts, and systems collapse. What endures are the relationships we cultivate. The children we nurture. The colleagues we mentor. The marketplace participants we serve with integrity. The friends who walk with us through grief. The neighbours who share a meal. The prayers whispered on our behalf. These are the accounts that remain open long after the ledgers of this world are closed.

Writing this book has been, for me, an act of gratitude. Gratitude to my mother, who prayed me into strength. Gratitude to my family, who stood with me. Gratitude to mentors and colleagues, who believed in me. Gratitude to marketplace participants and teams, who trusted me. Gratitude to unsung heroes, the cleaners, the assistants, the guards, who reminded me of dignity in every role. Gratitude to God, who has never left me.

Every chapter is a thank you. Every story is a tribute. Every insight is a seed I pray will grow in others.

And now, as I close these pages, I think not only of my own story, but of yours. Because this is not only my testimony. It is an invitation. To see relationships as wealth. To invest in them as diligently as we invest in accounts. To guard them as fiercely as we guard assets. To celebrate them as joyfully as we celebrate dividends. To let them be the compass that guides us through life's storms.

The future will demand many things of us. But above all, it will demand hearts for relationships. Hearts that are soft enough to empathise, strong enough to endure, wise enough to discern, generous enough to multiply. Hearts that refuse to let the world harden them. Hearts that believe love is not weakness, but strength.

That is my prayer for you, dear reader. That, as you close this book, you open your heart wider. That you look at your balance sheet and count differently, not just money, but memories; not just profits, but people; not just titles, but trust. That you build legacy accounts not only of wealth, but of wisdom and love. That you carry forward the conviction that the world's real capital is not in banks or markets, but in relationships. Because at the end of it all, when positions end, when portfolios close, when achievements are forgotten, what will remain is the love we gave, the trust we built, the people we carried, and the God who carried us. That is relational wealth. That is legacy, that is life and that has always been, and will always be, my heart for relationships.

CHAPTER 33

The Hidden Wealth of the Invisible Worker

Not all leadership carries a title. Not every sacrifice is seen. Not every decision is made in a marketplace. Yet some of the most influential women I've known lead from kitchen tables, hospital corridors, WhatsApp prayer groups, and quiet corners where no one claps, but heaven sees.

We have inherited a culture that often defines leadership as public visibility, microphones, strategy sessions, and polished bios. But many of the women who hold communities together, who counsel through casseroles and intercede through tears, are doing Kingdom work without applause. And they are rich in relational wealth.

I think of my mother, her worn-out hands preparing food for guests she didn't invite but never turned away. Her prayers whispered over sleeping children. Her quiet strength that held a household through financial strain, emotional storms, and unspoken grief. No podium ever held her name, but she led. Faithfully. Fiercely. Fruitfully.

These are the women I want to honour. The ones who wake early to make school lunches, who manage their ageing parents' medications, who work full shifts and still show up to serve in church. The ones who remind a grieving friend to eat. Who plans the family funeral while still nursing their own heartbreak? Who remembers every birthday, every detail, every silent burden of those they love.

They are mothers, aunties, sisters, nannies, caregivers, deacons, encouragers. Their ministry is not platformed, but it is powerful.

We need to redefine leadership. Leadership is influence. It is responsibility. It is impact. And if a woman is shaping character, holding space, lifting others, she is leading. Period. Jesus noticed invisible women. The bleeding woman who touched His robe. The widow who gave two coins. The Samaritan at the well. Each encounter dignified what society had overlooked. He didn't just preach to crowds; He stopped for the unseen.

I've watched women lead from the margins, leading healing in families, restoration in churches, wisdom in times of crisis. I've sat in rooms where no "leaders" were present, and yet the woman speaking spoke with such clarity and spiritual depth that I knew I was in the presence of true authority. So many of these women ask, "Am I doing enough?" My answer is: you are doing more than enough. You are doing sacred work.

Relational wealth is not just about high-level connections. It's about the trust you've built over years. The tears you've wiped. The meals you've shared. The faith you've passed down. That is legacy.

That is leadership. To every invisible worker: we see you. We honour you. You are not invisible to heaven.

Let us lift our definition of leadership to include the silent builders, the emotional anchors, the peacemakers, the servers. For theirs is the hidden wealth that sustains families, churches, and entire communities.

"She rises while it is yet night and provides food for her household... Strength and dignity are her clothing." - Proverbs 31

This is the hidden wealth of the invisible worker. And it is priceless.

www.ingramcontent.com/pod-product-compliance
Lightning Source LLC
Chambersburg PA
CBHW071259220526
45468CB00001B/191